NatureWalks

AND

Sunday Drives

'ROUND EDMONTON

Henry Saley

Don H. Meredith

Harry Stelfox

Dave Ealey

Edmonton
Natural History
Club

The Publisher:

Edmonton Natural History Club
Box 1582
Edmonton, Alberta T5J 2N9

Canadian Cataloguing in Publication Data

Saley, Henry, 1953-.

Nature Walks & Sunday Drives 'Round Edmonton

     ISBN #0-9698507-2-7 (pbk.)

Graphic Design & Layout: Broken Arrow Solutions Incorporated

Cover Photographs: Gordon Court

Black-and-white illustrations: Gary Ross

Cartography: Trevor Wiens & Broken Arrow Solutions Incorporated

Printing: Quebecor World Jasper

Preface

A lot has changed since Joy and Cam Finlay penned the preface to the first edition in 1995.

The City of Edmonton and surrounding communities have continued to grow, expanding into more natural areas and agricultural lands. With more people come more demands on resources. Some of those resources include places to go to relax and truly recreate ourselves while enjoying the natural world and its inhabitants. Fortunately, many Edmontonians realize the values of these places and groups like the Edmonton Natural History Club have been working hard to preserve them and educate others about them.

Other changes since 1995 include the loss of the provincial Watchable Wildlife program as a result of government cutbacks. The program was established in 1988 to encourage "the growing public interest in wildlife viewing and nature appreciation." Although the program was discontinued, many viewing sites were developed and many are still maintained by local volunteers, including some mentioned here. Another change that occurred was the advancement of the World Wide Web of the Internet. Much of the wildlife information that was available in print from government and non-government organizations is now available to the world on the web. In this revised edition, we have added addresses to web sites as they relate to the locations listed here. Web addresses do change over time. So, if you have trouble with one, use one of the many search engines to find the information you require.

We have added a new site and two auto tours to this edition. Matchayaw (Devil's) Lake is located west of Edmonton and includes Imrie Park, an excellent place to observe waterfowl and other wildlife. The Battle Lake Auto Tour takes you through the parkland and farm country southwest of the city. The Big Lake – Matchayaw (Devil's) Lake Auto Tour, explores some interesting sites in the Glory Hills west of the city.

The popularity of the first edition of this guide and the publication of this second edition reconfirms the value Edmontonians and visitors to Edmonton place in the natural areas in and nearby the city. They are there for all to enjoy while pondering the variety of ways there are to make a living in this world.

BY DON H. MEREDITH [JUNE 2003]

Preface

Having been explorers of nature in and around Edmonton for nearly 40 years, we are delighted to see so many familiar places featured in this first guide to nature-viewing sites in the Edmonton region. We never cease to marvel at the unique aspects of landforms, the character of wildlife communities and the richness of seasons that typify each special place. And no matter how often we go to each place, there is always something we've never seen before. It takes a book like this to help identify and describe the valuable natural areas within and close to our ever-growing urban centre. It takes a book like this to also demonstrate that, although nature may be all around us, space must be saved for the natural world to be sustained. As a result of cumulative efforts by individuals and organizations, natural areas have begun to be protected.

In Elk Island National Park, a cross-country skier can view the largest land mammal in North America. And for the record, the smallest land mammal in North America is also found there. In between the largest wood bison and the smallest pygmy shrew, you can find moose, elk and deer, all at home in the only national park with a fence around it.

Besides being the chickadee capital of the world, according to annual bird counts, Edmonton has one of the highest concentrations of black-billed magpies. Merlins, which occupy the magpies' abandoned twig nests, thrive here because of the abundance of waxwings, which in turn thrive on all the berries of mountain ashes that have been planted in city yards and have spread into the river valley. For all things there is a reason; the cause-and-effect connections between the sun, rain, us, you, plants, animals and all of nature just keep us exploring in thought long after we have walked a trail.

The publication of this guidebook is a happy event, for it further confirms a value we hold of having natural places for all to enjoy. Even more, we are thankful that protected natural places are there to be featured in a book. It is proof that, as a society, we are starting to become caring stewards of the natural treasures in our environment, for our own sake and for the sake of nature too.

Whether wandering in a poplar bush, skiing through spruce woods, walking on a boardwalk in a muskeg, or paddling around a big slough or lake, enjoy!

BY JOY AND CAM FINLAY [MARCH 1995]

Table of Contents

Introduction Take a Nature Break 1
Who Can Use This Guide? 2
Tips for Watching Wildlife With Respect 2
How to Use This Guide 3
Symbols Legend 5

Edmonton Area Nature Almanac 6

City of Edmonton Viewing Sites Edmonton River Valley Parks 8
John Janzen Nature Centre 10
Whitemud Ravine 10
William Hawrelak Park 12
Victoria Park 12
Kinsmen Park 13
Mill Creek Park 14
Gold Bar Park 15

West of Edmonton Viewing Sites Battle Lake (Alberta 4-H Centre) 18
Chickakoo Lake Recreation Area 20
Clifford E. Lee Nature Sanctuary 22
Coyote Lake Nature Sanctuary 24
Devonian Botanic Garden (University of Alberta) 26
Hasse Lake Provincial Park 28
Matchayaw (Devil's) Lake 30
St. Albert – Sturgeon River
(Big Lake, Red Willow Park and River Lot 56) 32
Wabamun Lake 34
Wagner Natural Area 36

East of Edmonton Viewing Sites Beaverhill Lake (Tofield) 40
Blackfoot Recreation Area 42
Dow Wildlife Greenbelt Viewing Area 44
Elk Island National Park 46
Halfmoon Lake Natural Area 48
Miquelon Lake Provincial Park 50
Sherwood Park Natural Area 52
Strathcona Wilderness Centre 54
Telford Lake (Leduc) 56

Auto Tours Battle Lake Auto Tour 58
Big Lake – Matchayaw Lake Auto Tour 62
Wabamun Lake – Lac Ste. Anne Auto Tour 66
Cooking Lake Moraine Auto Tour 70
Gwynne Outlet Auto Tour 74

Sources for Further Information Agency and Organization Contacts 78
Editor's Choice of References 78

Corporate Sponsors

The production of this second edition of *Nature Walks and Sunday Drives 'Round Edmonton* has been assisted by the generous financial support of our corporate sponsors as shown below.

Alberta Sport, Recreation, Parks and Wildlife Foundation:

Alberta
Sport Recreation
Parks & Wildlife
Foundation

supporting the development of parks; recreation programs and services; and the management, conservation and preservation of fish and wildlife.

Federation of Alberta Naturalists:

the voice of Alberta naturalists— promoting the enjoyment, study and conservation of Alberta's natural history.

Enbridge – Community Based Environmental Initiative Program:

helping local groups to take action on their commitment to environmental protection, conservation and public awareness.

Alberta Ecotrust Foundation:

a unique partnership of corporations, environmental organizations and individuals that supports environmental action at the community level.

Acknowledgements

This book is the result of a cooperative effort involving a large number of committed individuals from several naturalist and non-government organizations, as well as from municipal, provincial and federal government agencies. Contributors provided advice, attended planning meetings, reviewed draft materials and field-checked viewing sites and auto tour routes—often on their own time and at their own expense. The following individuals were actively involved in the project in one way or another, mostly in a volunteer capacity.

John Acorn
Elisabeth Beaubien
Roger Bryan
Tom Cameron
Ross Chapman
Murray Christman
Dick Clayton
Pat Clayton
Patsy Cotterill
Gord Court
Doug Culbert
Patti Danos
Peter Demulder
Richard DeSmet
Loney Dickson
Dave Doze
John Folinsbee
Jean Funk
Alice Hendry
Alan Hingston
Geoff Holroyd
Tanya Hope
Doris Hopkins
Eric Hopkins
Derek Johnson
Jackie Kallal
Keith Kivett

Bob Lane
Jim Lange
Gerry Lunn
Ray Makowecki
Andy McCracken
Allen McQueen
Sandy Myers
Wayne Nordstrom
Doug Nothstein
Sandra Opdenkamp
Claire Radke
Marg Reine
Bill Reynolds
Martin Sawdon
Manny Schmidt
Glen Semenchuk
Carol Smith
Brad Stelfox
Randy Strocki
Tom Sutherland
Bruce Turner
Judy Vance
Kirsten van der Meer
Cindy Verbeek
Dennis Verbeek
Dave Westworth
Ed Whitelock

For the first edition (1995), Claire Radke and David Doyle were the primary researchers and compilers of background information on viewing sites and auto tour routes. Henry Saley (Orchis

Communications Design) was the principal writer. Trevor Weins prepared the maps. For the second edition (2003), Don Meredith (Don H. Meredith Professional Writing Services) provided research, writing and editorial services, while Judy Cook (Broken Arrow Solutions Inc.) provided graphic design and layout services, as well as enhancements to most of the maps. The production of the second edition was under the direction of a steering committee consisting of Dave Ealey, Tanya Hope and Harry Stelfox.

HARRY STELFOX
Project Manager

Introduction

Take a Nature Break

Explore over 25 of the best watchable wildlife spots in and around Edmonton. It's a great way to be active, spend time with family and friends and leave behind everyday stresses. The more you experience the natural world, the more you'll get hooked on discovering new sites. This guide covers the Edmonton viewing region, as outlined in the following map.

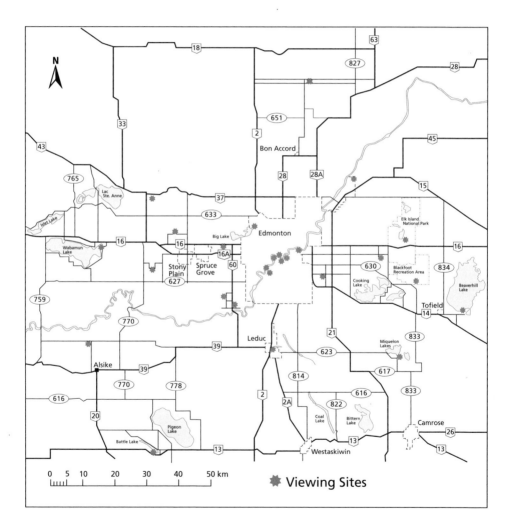

Who Can Use This Guide?

Whether you're young, or a senior, in a group or on your own, you'll find this guide a good start to finding the animals, plants and landscapes that make up Edmonton and the surrounding area.

Most sites (except some stops on the auto tours) have well-marked access, good parking and developed trails.

Tips for Watching Wildlife With Respect

For best summer viewing success, visit during mornings or early evenings.
Midday is a time when most wildlife are resting or just staying out of the heat. However, if that's the most convenient time for you, there are still some terrific things to be seen. Wildflowers and butterflies are at their best during midday and some animals are active from dawn to dusk.

Move slowly and quietly.
Animals are always aware of potential danger. They assume you intend to make a meal of them. Try sitting quietly on a bench or log for several minutes. The surrounding wildlife will become more accustomed to your presence and may then go about their normal activities.

Stay on developed trails as much as possible.
Trails are for trampling on—the undergrowth is not. Healthy undergrowth is critical for animal food and shelter. Animals adapt to a regular flow of people along a trail, but too many people in unexpected places may cause them to move out of an area.

Keep a respectful distance.
If the animal stays alert to your presence, you are too close. Your respect and common sense can ensure that new young are raised and not abandoned. Some animals, like pelicans, may never return if disturbed too often.

Bring binoculars and field guides.
You can certainly enjoy yourself with minimal equipment. However, binoculars will give you a better view of those elusive animals on a lake, high in a tree or across a wide meadow. Field guides will help you to identify the plants and animals. Suggested resources are listed at the end of each site description and at the back of this guide.

Go a step further than just spotting and identifying.
If you can identify what you see, that's rewarding. To get even more enjoyment, watch the behaviour of birds and other wildlife. You'll soon know not just what they look like and what their names are, but where they are commonly found, what they eat, how they move and other interesting things about the way they live.

Watch and listen for animal signs.
Finding telltale signs of animal activity can be as rewarding as seeing the animals themselves. Look for trails, nests, tracks, browse (chewed plants), tunnels in wood, burrows and droppings. Animal droppings are surprisingly easy to identify (see reference section, page 79). Listen for the territorial and breeding calls of birds, frogs and other wildlife, especially at springtime.

Carry a notebook to record your discoveries.
You'll be amazed at how a few notes here and there will add up to a fine record of your outdoor adventures. Try keeping a journal of your sightings throughout the year, including dates, locations and interesting behaviours. Your notes may interest other naturalists, biologists and site managers.

Be considerate of the environment.
Leave viewing sites, including plants and animals, undamaged by your visits. Be sure your garbage is properly disposed or recycled. Many wildlife viewing sites are **User Maintained**, therefore pack out what you pack in. Return used brochures to kiosks for re-use.

Control pets.
Pets can harm wildlife and hinder viewing opportunities. They should be under your control at all times, or better yet, left at home or in your vehicle.

How to Use This Guide

Viewing Sites

1. Choose a site from the Table of Contents and check the overview map at the beginning of the section that incorporates the site.

2. Each site description introduces a few commonly seen features and some special ones. Keep in mind that this description is only a small sample of what each site has to offer. Detailed site maps and other brochures, available at many sites, through site sponsors or off the web, will give you more information. Refer also to "Suggested readings for more discovery" at the end of each site description.

3. Symbols beside each site map indicate facilities that are available and activities that are supported. Refer to the symbols legend on page 5.

4. "Things to do" focuses on those activities that are friendly to the environment and compatible with wildlife viewing. Some sites have various facilities for recreation. Call the contact telephone number for more information.

Auto Tours

Auto tours provide a self-guiding route by which you can visit a few viewing sites and other points of interest on a one-day outing from

Edmonton. Interesting features and stops are pointed out along the way.

1. Choose an auto tour from the Table of Contents.

2. Review the overview map at the beginning of each tour description.

3. The tours give choices for stopping at several sites along the way. Based on the time you wish to spend, choose the sites that are right for you. You can certainly plan to do the tours more than once, stopping at different sites each trip. We suggest taking along an up-to-date road map or, better still, an access map at a scale of 1:250 000 (available from map specialty and some outdoor stores).

Country Highways and Roads

Each major highway (primary or secondary) in Alberta is identified in the text of this guide by the abbreviation "Hwy." followed by its number, for example: Hwy. 16, Hwy. 799. The lesser country roads are identified in the province by a system of numbers based on the Alberta Land Survey, such as Twp. Rd. 524 or Rge. Rd. 43. Although this numbering system may seem haphazard to the casual traveller, it is actually quite helpful in determining where you are in Alberta.

"Twp. Rd." is the abbreviation used on most maps for "Township Road." Township roads are those roads running east and west between townships in the surveyed portion of the province. Townships are six-mile by six-mile parcels of land that are arranged in north-south columns called "Ranges." Township roads are numbered from south to north, starting at the United States border, based on 10 plus the number of kilometres the particular road is from that border. Because the townships were originally surveyed using the old system of miles instead of kilometres, the number of the road may not represent the actual distance to the border, but it will be close. So, Twp. Rd. 524 is roughly 514 kilometres in a straight line from the U.S. border.

"Rge. Rd." is the abbreviation for "Range Road," except on maps herein where "R.R." refers to "Range Roads." These roads run generally north and south. Range roads are numbered from east to west beginning at the major north-south longitudinal meridians used to start the land surveys. In Alberta those meridians are the 4th Meridian (Alberta-Saskatchewan border, 110 degrees west longitude), the 5th Meridian (114 degrees, through Stony Plain) and the 6th Meridian (118 degrees). These roads are numbered based on 10 plus the number of kilometres from the meridian. So, Rge. Rd. 14 just west of Stony Plain is roughly 4 kilometres from the 5th Meridian, whereas Rge. Rd. 10 is the 5th Meridian. Range Roads east of Stony Plain are counted from the Saskatchewan border. Thus, from the road numbers, you can determine that the junction of Twp. Rd. 540 and Rge. Rd. 270 in the Stony Plain area is roughly 530 kilometres from the U.S. border and 260 kilometres from the Saskatchewan border.

Symbols Legend

FACILITIES AND ACTIVITIES

Boat Launch

Brochure/Checklists

Canoe Launch

Cycling

Entry Fee

Fishing

Guided Tour

Hiking/Walking Trail

Interpretive Displays/ Programs

Observation Platform/ Viewpoint

Picnic/Day Use

Picnic Shelter

Self-guided Trail

Swimming

Tent Camping

Toilets

Trail Riding

Wheelchair Accessible*

X-Country Skiing

*Wheelchair accessibility is indicated only for those sites that have been designated as such by the responsible site management authority. Access for parking and washrooms should be good, but access to the trail system may be variable and localized. Phone the appropriate site information contact for further details.

Edmonton Area

JANUARY | Snowy owls are often seen in the countryside, perching on power poles and fence posts—keeping a watchful eye for mice and voles.

FEBRUARY | Listen for the yodeling and yipping of coyotes on a clear night—they become more vocal during their breeding season.

MARCH | Black-capped chickadees begin to excavate nest cavities and the first crows return—sure signs of spring. Mating season begins for red squirrels, as groups of males chase receptive females through the trees.

APRIL | Attend the Snow Goose Festival at Beaverhill Lake to view thousands of geese: snows, Canadas and greater white-fronts.

MAY | Listen to wood frogs "quacking" their spring breeding calls from flooded ditches and marshy areas.

JUNE | A profusion of white blossoms cover choke cherry, pin cherry and saskatoon shrubs in the river valley and adjacent ravines.

JULY | This month is butterfly season and the river valley is a-flutter with sulphurs, blues, anglewings, and skippers. To learn more, join one of several butterfly counts in the Edmonton region.

AUGUST | The southern migration of shorebirds and warblers peaks, as does the bird banding activity at the Beaverhill Bird Observatory.

SEPTEMBER | The smell of ripened high-bush cranberry in aspen woods is a sure sign of fall—also a good time to search out various types of mushrooms. Territorial battles between individual red squirrels heat up as young-of-the-year seek territories of their own.

OCTOBER | Large flocks of ducks and geese can be seen making flights to and from water bodies and grain fields in preparation for the fall migration.

NOVEMBER | White-tailed deer begin their breeding season or rut in which both does and bucks can be seen moving about at any time of the day. Project Feeder Watch begins for those who wish to monitor their bird feeders on a regular basis and report their observations—contact the John Janzen Nature Centre for more details.

DECEMBER | Join the Edmonton Christmas Bird Count by contacting the John Janzen Nature Centre—a good time for a family outing and to meet other naturalists.

City of Edmonton

[VIEWING SITES]

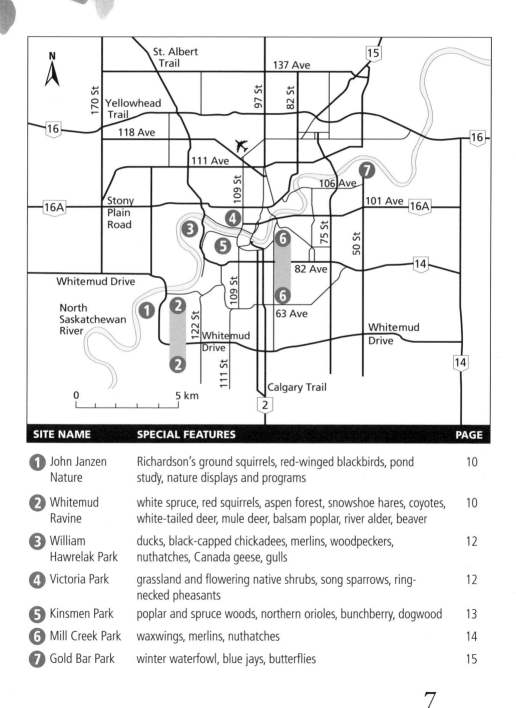

SITE NAME	SPECIAL FEATURES	PAGE
❶ John Janzen Nature	Richardson's ground squirrels, red-winged blackbirds, pond study, nature displays and programs	10
❷ Whitemud Ravine	white spruce, red squirrels, aspen forest, snowshoe hares, coyotes, white-tailed deer, mule deer, balsam poplar, river alder, beaver	10
❸ William Hawrelak Park	ducks, black-capped chickadees, merlins, woodpeckers, nuthatches, Canada geese, gulls	12
❹ Victoria Park	grassland and flowering native shrubs, song sparrows, ring-necked pheasants	12
❺ Kinsmen Park	poplar and spruce woods, northern orioles, bunchberry, dogwood	13
❻ Mill Creek Park	waxwings, merlins, nuthatches	14
❼ Gold Bar Park	winter waterfowl, blue jays, butterflies	15

THINGS TO DO:

- check into educational and recreational programs available for families, birthday parties, conventions and other groups

- take part in a special event organized by a parks leader

- enroll your children in a spring or summer day camp

- visit one of the interpretive facilities: John Janzen Nature Centre, Fort Edmonton Park, Provincial Museum, Valley Zoo, John Walter Museum

- angle for fish along the river; catch and release is recommended

- bicycle, jog or picnic along the Capital City Park trails

- join with members of the Edmonton Bird Club or the Edmonton Natural History Club to participate in Christmas Bird Counts, May Species Counts and field trips

- pick up brochures for cross-country ski trails, fishing and cycling at a City of Edmonton facility.

Edmonton River Valley Parks

In the early days of Edmonton's history, the city leaders identified the river valley and adjacent ravines for preservation. Today, the park system extends for about 40 km through the centre of the city. The main hiking trails follow the river valley with secondary trails extending into numerous connecting ravines. Trails link park areas throughout the city to create one of the largest urban green belts in North America. Though previously disturbed by settlement, mining and lumbering, the river valley is slowly returning to a natural state and becoming valuable parkland for wildlife and people.

Special features

Spring and fall are great times to watch for thousands of birds that use the river valley as a migration corridor. Bald eagles, which are more like scavengers than predators, patrol the river for dead fish washed onshore. Ring-billed gulls, returning from as far as Mexico, are very noticeable along the riverbanks in late March. Flycatchers, thrushes, vireos and warblers pass through in large numbers during mid-May. Some of them stay to nest in the valley. These songbirds begin heading south in August. Sandhill cranes fly noisily overhead in September, on their way to California and farther south.

Red squirrels are year-round residents of the city and river valley. Unlike most other mammals, these bold denizens of our forests advertise their presence to all intruders of their territories. Unlike ground squirrels and chipmunks, red squirrels do not hibernate and work hard all winter to find sufficient food.

Great horned owls begin nesting as early as February in the ravines. By the time spring leaves begin unfolding in early May, the young owls are departing nests to explore their nearby world.

Peregrine falcons nest on the AGT Toll Building in the centre of Edmonton at 100 Street and 102 Avenue, the Clinical Sciences Building beside the Mackenzie Health Sciences Centre (U of A campus), the Inland Cement Plant overlooking Yellowhead Trail, the Beverly railroad trestle overlooking Yellowhead Trail, and on the Imperial Oil flaring stack at 34 St. and Baseline Road. The best peregrine viewing is probably at the Clinical Sciences Building, looking up from the picnic/lunch area east of the main entrance to the Health Sciences Centre. Edmonton has had as many as four pairs of peregrines breeding at the above sites in any one summer, more than any other Canadian city.

White-tailed deer frequent the river valley and park areas. Although not as common as white tails, mule deer may also be seen, especially during the rut for both species in November and early December.

The black-billed magpie is a handsome and common bird in Edmonton. A world record (3374 magpies) was tallied during the city's 2001 Christmas Bird Count. This year-round resident prefers to live in areas settled by people. It scavenges road kills and feeds on worms, grasshoppers, and many insects that we consider harmful.

Black-capped chickadees also occur in record numbers in Edmonton. They are dependable companions on any outing. If you're patient, you might entice them to take sunflower seeds right out of your outstretched hand. In spring, listen for their mating song: a long and sweetly melancholy "here, sweetie."

SUGGESTED READINGS FOR MORE DISCOVERY:

Cycle Edmonton - Map, Information and Trail Guide, City of Edmonton, available online through www.gov.edmonton.ab.ca.

Ski Sense winter brochure – General Information and Ski Area Maps, City of Edmonton, available online through www.gov.edmonton.ab.ca.

Urban Fishing Brochure. City of Edmonton.

Edmonton Naturalist. Journal of the Edmonton Natural History Club, published three times a year.

FOR MORE INFORMATION, CONTACT:

City of Edmonton
Park Rangers
Phone: (780) 496-2950

Nature Information Line (John Janzen Nature Centre)
Phone: (780) 496-8787
Web site: through www.gov.edmonton.ab.ca

Northern Alberta Bird Hotline number: 433-BIRD

Alberta Sustainable Resource Development's Fishing in Alberta web site – www3.gov.ab.ca/srd/fw/fishing/

GETTING THERE:
Exit from Whitemud Drive
to Fox Drive and watch for
the directional signs to Fort
Edmonton Park and the
John Janzen Nature Centre.
For more information,
telephone – (780) 496-
2925; web – through
www.gov.edmonton.ab.ca.

RICHARDSON'S
GROUND SQUIRREL

GETTING THERE:
Exit from Fox Drive to
Keillor Road, drive around
the picnic area and back
under the bridge over
Whitemud Creek, or

Exit from Whitemud
Freeway at 122 Street
heading south and take
access road to Rainbow
Valley Park.

John Janzen Nature Centre

Special features

Knowledgeable staff, public events, live animal displays and a self-guiding trail make this facility a logical place to start experiencing nature in the city. Richardson's ground squirrels scurry across the open grass as you approach the centre. In late summer, they collect seeds to store in underground chambers, but since they are winter hibernators, they may not use this food until spring. A small pond and a marsh, created adjacent to the nature centre, attract easily spotted ducks, songbirds and wood frogs. Ask at the nature centre for small nets and field guides for catching and identifying "mini-beasts" from the pond waters. Always return your catch to the pond.

Whitemud Ravine

Whitemud Ravine gives a feeling of wilderness in the city. This picturesque ravine carves up to 60 m deep from the southwest edge of the city through to the river valley. The ravine features a small meandering creek and contains the highest diversity of plants and animals in the city. Nine kilometres of trails lead you through changing scenes of forests, open fields and bottomlands along the creek.

Special features

White spruce forests offer a cool and protected shelter for many animals. Up in the trees, red squirrels chatter from a safe distance. They are agitated by your intrusion into their territory. Look for their mossy summer nests built high in a spruce tree and for discarded cone scales that form piles, called middens, on the ground. In the winter, their tracks are the ones that always lead from tree to tree. During really cold days, they

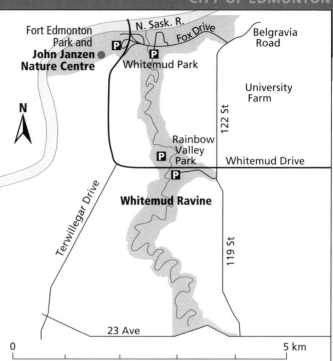

Fort Edmonton Park and **John Janzen Nature Centre**

N. Sask. R.

Fox Drive

Belgravia Road

Whitemud Park

University Farm

122 St

N

Rainbow Valley Park

Whitemud Drive

Whitemud Ravine

Terwillegar Drive

119 St

23 Ave

0   5 km

John Janzen Nature Centre Only

stay warm in underground dens.

Aspen forests permit light to filter through their leaves, allowing a lush growth of wildflowers and shrubs. The snowshoe hare snips away this undergrowth along its travel highways. These runways are especially noticeable in winter. Look closely at hare tracks and note the huge size difference between the front and hind feet. Where a hare has been resting or feeding, you'll find tan-coloured droppings (bunny buttons) left behind.

In soft, moist areas of ground, you'll see the tracks of white-tailed and mule deer. Stay quiet when exploring the ravine in the early morning or at dusk, and you'll have a good chance of seeing these graceful animals feeding along the forest edge. In the winter, they munch the tender twigs of shrubs such as red-osier dogwood and willows.

Balsam poplar and river alder are common along the creek because they grow so well in wet soil. In the fall, look for large clusters of freshly cut twigs and branches in the water. Beaver store these food caches to survive the winter. A beaver can cut through a good-sized poplar in a matter of 20 minutes, if uninterrupted. To make up for continual wear, its strong "buck" teeth (incisors) grow continuously. Grassy meadows have likely been cleared of trees by beaver.

RED SQUIRREL

11

City of Edmonton

[VIEWING SITES]

GETTING THERE:
Exit from Groat Road, on south side of the river and follow signs to William Hawrelak Park.

William Hawrelak Park

Would you believe that more dollars are spent worldwide on sand and gravel than on gold, platinum or diamonds? Not surprisingly then, sand and gravel are Alberta's most valuable mineral resources, next to oil! Hawrelak Park is situated on a former extraction site that supplied sand and gravel for building bridges, roads, airports and other such city projects, from the early 1900s on. This extraction site was reclaimed as a park with grassy expanses, trees and a pond. Waterfowl offer a great opportunity for photography in this area because they are unusually tame from being fed by people. However, feeding wildlife may do some harm by upsetting their normal diet. The man-made lake and its islands attract Canada geese, mallards and common goldeneyes.

MALLARD

GETTING THERE:
Trails begin at the top of the riverbank at Ezio Faraone Park adjacent the High Level Bridge or down a stairway at Le Marchand Mansion at 116th St. and 100th Ave. Free parking is available at Victoria Park just off the River Valley Road in the valley bottom.

Victoria Park

If you live or work near the city centre, take a nature break in the river valley. Grassland, shrubs and patchy tree cover are typical of the sunny north side of the river valley. The slopes face south and receive direct sunlight, which creates a warm, dry environment. Flowering shrubs such as choke cherry, saskatoon and pin cherry attract a colourful and musical collection of songbirds. One of the first birds to arrive here in the spring is the lively song sparrow. It builds a nest on the ground or in a shrub. Throughout the summer, you'll find it scratching the ground for weed seeds.

CHOKE CHERRY

12

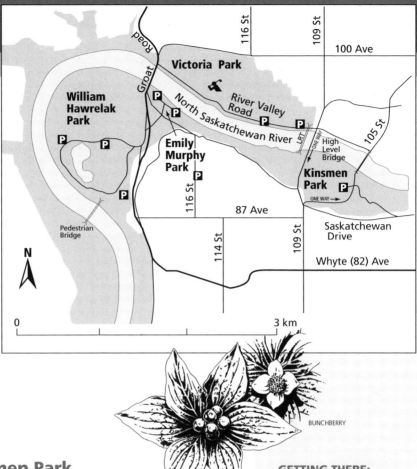

116 St

109 St

100 Ave

Groat Road

Victoria Park

River Valley Road

William Hawrelak Park

North Saskatchewan River

LRT

ONE WAY

High Level Bridge

105 St

Emily Murphy Park

116 St

Kinsmen Park

ONE WAY →

87 Ave

109 St

Saskatchewan Drive

Pedestrian Bridge

N

114 St

Whyte (82) Ave

0   3 km

BUNCHBERRY

Kinsmen Park

Wooded stands of balsam poplar mixed with spruce are typical of the south side of the river, where the environment of these north-facing banks is cool and moist. The tree cover is a good buffer against the noise from inner city traffic. Look for a flash of orange and black in the tops of poplar trees as northern orioles scour the branches for caterpillars and other insects. Bunchberries decorate the forest floor with their large white flower clusters in early summer. If you look closely, you'll see that the white "petals" are actually bracts (a type of leaf), which surround numerous tiny, white flowers clustered in the middle. The flowers develop into bright red berries in late summer.

GETTING THERE:

Park at the Kinsmen Sports Centre by the 105th St. bridge (east side of site) or at Emily Murphy Park just east of the Groat Road bridge (west end of site). Trails begin from the top of the valley at the south end of the High Level Bridge and also from Saskatchewan Drive just above the LRT tunnel to the university. A pedestrian/cycle path under the LRT bridge lets you cross the river to Victoria Park.

13

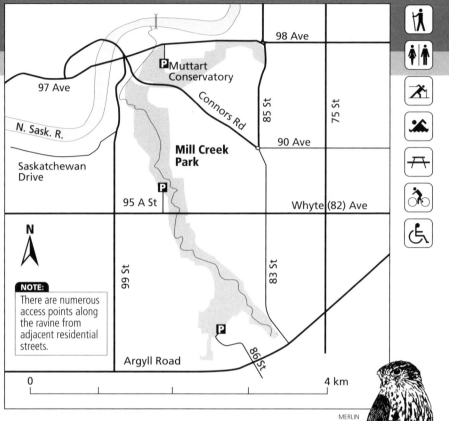

98 Ave

P Muttart
Conservatory

97 Ave

Connors Rd

85 St

75 St

N. Sask. R.

90 Ave

Mill Creek
Park

Saskatchewan
Drive

P

95 A St

Whyte (82) Ave

N

99 St

83 St

NOTE:
There are numerous
access points along
the ravine from
adjacent residential
streets.

P

Argyll Road

86 St

0   4 km

MERLIN

GETTING THERE:

Parking is available by the
swimming pool at 95A St.
north of 82nd Ave., at
Muttart Conservatory in the
main river valley and by the
Velodrome near 86 St. and
Argyll Road.

Mill Creek Park

Mixed forests of white
spruce, aspen, balsam
poplar and birch attract a
variety of birds, including
blue jays, Bohemian
waxwings and brown
creepers.

Bohemian waxwings feed on the abundant fruit
trees planted in the city, especially the bright
orange berries of the mountain ash. More than
16 000 waxwings have been counted during some
winters! Merlins are able to stay in the city year-
round by feeding on overwintering waxwings and
resident house sparrows. These small but feisty
falcons raise their young in old magpie nests.
More than 50 nesting pairs have been seen in the
city—the highest known breeding population of
any city in the world.

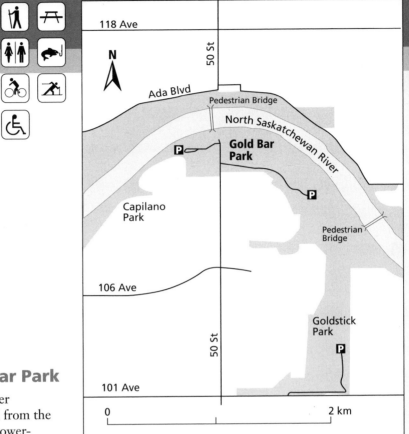

118 Ave

50 St

N

Ada Blvd

Pedestrian Bridge

North Saskatchewan River

P

Gold Bar Park

Capilano Park

P

Pedestrian Bridge

106 Ave

50 St

Goldstick Park

P

101 Ave

0   2 km

Gold Bar Park

Warm water discharged from the Rossdale power-generating plant keeps the river from freezing, making this a good birdwatching spot year-round. Hundreds of ducks, mostly mallard and common goldeneye, are spotted on the open water of the river during the annual Christmas Bird Count. Gyrfalcons can sometimes be seen chasing these overwintering ducks.

This park was named for the gravel bars at the mouth of Gold Bar Creek, where early miners panned for gold. From mid-May to July, many butterflies, including the Canadian tiger swallowtail, patrol the edges of Gold Bar Creek looking for mates. Blue jays frequent the park throughout the year. You may be puzzled by the origin of a very unusual bird call, only to find that the blue jay has fooled you again with a sound from its wide repertoire.

GETTING THERE:
Parking is reached from 50th Street on the south side of the river.

COMMON GOLDENEYE

15

West
of Edmonton

SITE NAME	DISTANCE FROM EDMONTON CITY CENTRE	SPECIAL FEATURES	PAGE
1 Battle Lake (Alberta 4-H Centre)	108 km SW	glacial drainage channel, ravines, fern glade, bald eagles, common loons, tree swallows, red-necked grebes, porcupines	18
2 Chickakoo Lake Recreation Area	39 km W	pitted delta, common loons, puddle ducks, diving ducks, beaver, muskrats, willow groves, mourning cloak butterflies	20
3 Clifford E. Lee Nature Sanctuary	33 km SW	marsh wrens, red-winged and yellow-headed blackbirds, blue darner dragonflies, black terns, water milfoil, sand dunes, tiger beetles	22
4 Coyote Lake Nature Sanctuary	94 km SW	common loons, great blue herons, marsh marigolds, cotton grass, common red paintbrush, western wood lilies	24
5 Devonian Botanic Garden (University of Alberta)	33 km SW	Plants of Alberta and Native Peoples' Garden, tamarack fen, boreal chickadees, hairy woodpeckers, horsetail, wild black currant	26
6 Hasse Lake Provincial Park	40 km W	brook sticklebacks, ruffed grouse, ruddy ducks, American coots, northern pocket gophers	28
7 Matchayaw (Devil's) Lake	46 km NW	wildlife viewing blind, mallard, scaups, green-winged teal, northern shoveler, Canada goose, muskegs, tamarack forest	30
8 St. Albert – Sturgeon River (Big Lake, Red Willow Park and River Lot 56)	14 km NW	tiger salamanders, wood frogs, northern pintails, tundra swans, ermine, warbling vireos	32
9 Wabamun Lake	65 km W	ospreys, common terns, belted kingfishers, great blue herons, pike, perch, white suckers, whitefish, bald eagles, gyrfalcons, winter waterfowl	34
10 Wagner Natural Area	22 km W	carnivorous plants, wood frogs, marl ponds, stonewort, brown moss, marsh marigolds, bog violets, western wood lilies, round-leaved orchids	36

16

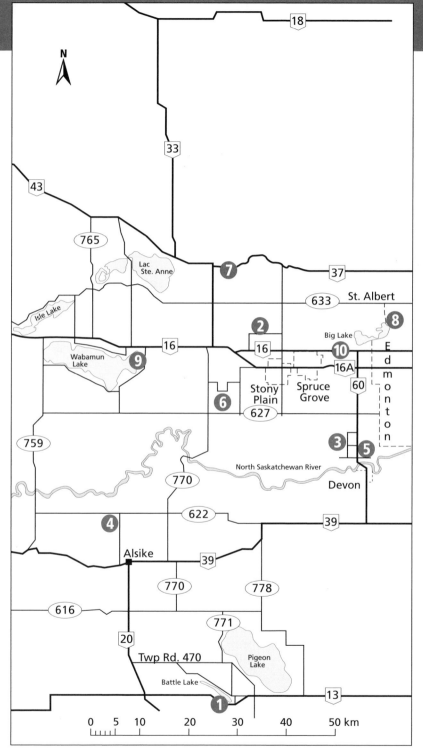

N

18

33

43

765

Lac Ste. Anne

7

37

633 St. Albert

Isle Lake

2

Big Lake

8

16

16

10

E
d
m
o
n
t
o
n

16A

Wabamun Lake

9

Stony Plain

Spruce Grove

60

6

627

3

5

759

North Saskatchewan River

770

Devon

622

39

4

Alsike

39

770

778

616

771

20

Twp Rd. 470

Pigeon Lake

Battle Lake

13

1

0 5 10   20   30   40   50 km

Battle Lake

BALD EAGLE

This privately owned site is operated by the Alberta 4-H Foundation. Visitors are welcome, but be sure to check in with the site managers upon your arrival to let them know of your presence and interests. During weekends in July and August, telephone beforehand.

Around 10 000 years ago, in this very spot, melting glaciers unleashed a torrent of water that carved a deep river valley. Today, the valley contains a long, deep and narrow lake—the headwaters of the Battle River. A hiking trail begins on the scenic edge of the valley, then drops suddenly into a cavernous ravine containing a lush forest of ferns and towering balsam poplars.

Special features

During a period of thousands of years, the ravine was gouged by a creek that now meanders into the lake. During spring runoff and summer floods, water gushes downstream with enough force to carry fallen trees and a great deal of sand, gravel and silt. Where the creek enters the lake, the flowing water suddenly slows and the suspended dirt finally settles. Over the years, the build-up of dirt has created a large area of fertile soil—a delta—on which the ferns and balsam poplars grow.

The fern glade is truly impressive. By midsummer, ostrich ferns stand over a metre tall. In the centre of the clumps of fronds are shorter, stiff, dark green leaves that become brown or blackish by late summer—these are the fertile fronds. They bear clusters of spore cases on the rolled-under leaf margins. Each cluster releases thousands of spores, some of which will land in suitable conditions to grow a new fern plant.

LOCATION:
108 km southwest of Edmonton city centre

SUGGESTED FIRST-TIME VIEWING:
1.5 hours to walk Fern Valley Trail and Porcupine Trail

THINGS TO DO:

- launch a canoe to explore more of this 7-km long lake
- hunt for different colours and textures of rocks along the streams (please leave the rocks for others to enjoy)
- book facilities and services for a group: dormitory, lodge with dining facilities and games room, archery, canoeing, baseball, volleyball, backcountry camping, fire circle, environmental appreciation programs and the Grant MacEwan Environmental Centre

SUGGESTED READINGS FOR MORE DISCOVERY:
Web – www.4H.ab.ca.

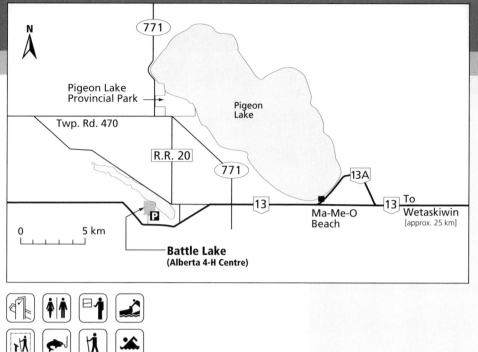

PORCUPINE

A cool, narrow gully exposes 65-million-year-old bedrock of sandstone and shale. This bedrock underlies the entire Battle Lake area. At the delta formed downstream of this gully, you get a terrific view of the lake. Bald eagles nest along the shore, but you're more likely to see common loons, red-necked grebes or tree swallows. With a sharp eye, you may spot an osprey, great blue heron or belted kingfisher, each with a unique talent for catching fish.

On the Porcupine Trail, your feet will sink into the mossy floor of the spruce forest. Here, porcupines have been busy girdling the bark from trees, with some trunks stripped clean. Look also for the trimmed twigs on red-osier dogwood and willow shrubs; these twigs are not pruned by shears but by the teeth of deer and moose.

FOR MORE INFORMATION, CONTACT:
4-H Foundation of Alberta
RR #1, Westerose, AB T0C 2V0
Phone: (780) 682-2153
E-mail: foundation@4hab.com

19

Chickakoo Lake

LOCATION:
39 km west of Edmonton city centre

SUGGESTED FIRST-TIME VIEWING:
Pick up a brochure at the Parkland County Centre, north of Stony Plain on Rge. Rd. 10 (5th Meridian), or online at www.parklandcounty.com. Take 1 hour to discover the natural features along Indian Ridge Trail.

THINGS TO DO:
- ride a mountain bike or hike the 14 km of maintained trails
- fish for brook trout (stocked annually)
- skate on the lake or cross-country ski during winter

SUGGESTED READINGS FOR MORE DISCOVERY:
Chickakoo Lake Trail Guide, County of Parkland, Recreation and Park Services.

Chickakoo Lake is part of the Glory Hills, a landscape created thousands of years ago when rivers from melting glaciers deposited large amounts of sand and silt. Chunks of glacial ice were buried in this "delta," leaving pits when the ice chunks melted. This landscape is called a pitted delta, with Chickakoo Lake occupying one of the pits. Today, the area is a 194-ha wildlife sanctuary of forest, lake and pond. The wooded trails follow the shoreline, giving a good view of lakeshore wildlife and plants.

Special features

Common loons nest on Chickakoo Lake, but since they need a large breeding territory, you are likely to see only one pair. You can distinguish them from ducks by their sharply pointed bill and larger, longer body. The call of the loon is a sound you never forget.

Ducks seen on the lakes and ponds are of two groups. Try to identify them:

The dabbling ducks, such as mallard and northern pintail, tip up to feed, mooning any passers-by. They take straight off from the water's surface when alarmed and usually swim with their tail held well above the water.

The diving ducks, such as bufflehead and common goldeneye, dive completely underwater to feed. They run along the surface of the water for a distance before lifting off and swim with their tails held close to the water.

Beaver are a symbol for Chickakoo Lake

BEAVER

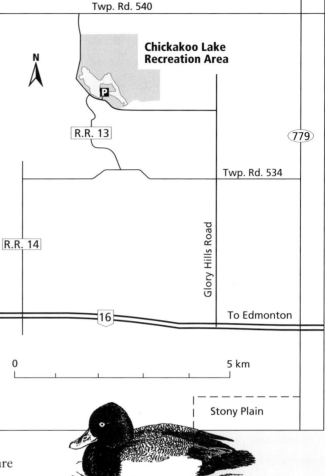

Twp. Rd. 540

Chickakoo Lake Recreation Area

N

P

R.R. 13

779

Twp. Rd. 534

Glory Hills Road

R.R. 14

16

To Edmonton

0   5 km

Stony Plain

LESSER SCAUP

since they seem to be active everywhere. Their lodges, built mostly with aspen branches, each take about a month to build and are used for many years. Other signs are felled trees, stumps and branches with large teeth marks. A natural timber faller, a beaver can fell over 200 trees a year. Not bad for one set of teeth. Beaver incisors continually grow to make up for the wear. A swimming muskrat is sometimes mistaken for a beaver. To tell them apart, remember that the muskrat is smaller and has a snake-like tail wriggling at the water's surface.

Willow groves are a common sight at the lake edge. In the spring, look for the fuzzy catkins (flowers). They often burst out before the leaves do, which lets the wind blow the pollen about and more effectively fertilize the female flowers. If that doesn't work, insects such as mourning cloak butterflies transfer pollen from flower to flower as they search for nectar.

FOR MORE INFORMATION, CONTACT:
The County of Parkland, Recreation and Park Services
Phone: (780) 968-8888
Web: www.parklandcounty. com

Alberta Sustainable Resource Development's *Fishing in Alberta* web site:
www3.gov.ab.ca/srd/fw/ fishing/

21

Clifford E. Lee

[N A T U R E   S A N C T U A R Y]

LOCATION:
33 km southwest of
Edmonton city centre

**SUGGESTED
FIRST-TIME VIEWING:**
1.5 hours to hike the
boardwalk

THINGS TO DO:
- join an informal walk of
  the trails with a naturalist
  group
- take a school or youth
  group for pond study
  along the boardwalk

**SUGGESTED READINGS
FOR MORE DISCOVERY:**
Local volunteers have
developed a series of
brochure guides for
interpreting the pond life,
waterfowl, insects and other
features. These are available
upon request to the site
managers.

Watch how the assortment of plants changes completely as you move from aspen woods to marsh, then to meadow and finally to the sandy soils of a pine forest. This variety of habitat attracts a diverse and abundant wildlife community that is remarkably lush for such a compact site. The boardwalk makes for terrific viewing of the marsh world—a habitat that teems with animals and vegetation.

Special features

Look for the following as you walk along the boardwalk that weaves through the marsh:

Marsh wrens have a distinctive musical rattle. Look for their ball-shaped nests woven into the stems of cattails up to a metre above the water.

Red-winged and yellow-headed blackbirds build their cup-shaped nests in much the same way. In spring, listen for the red-winged males belting out "O-ka-ree-a" as they sway precariously on top of a cattail. Compared to the bright colours of the males, the females might be considered boring to look at. However, their streaked, dark colours blend in very well with their surroundings: a handy feature when they sit on a nest.

Blue darner dragonflies, among the largest insects in Alberta, feed on mosquitoes and other flying insects. Be nice to them. A single dragonfly can wolf down 133 mosquitoes a day.

Black terns skim over the open water of the marsh. Watching them, you would think they spent their entire lives in the air! This tern snaps up insects as it flies.

Look into the clear water in early spring to see bright-green plant balls lying on the bottom. These are the winter buds of water milfoil, a feathery aquatic plant. The buds soon sprout, roots form and a new season's growth begins.

YELLOW-HEADED
BLACKBIRD

22

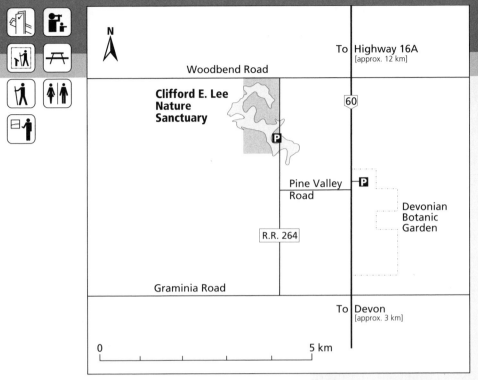

Sand dunes make up the soil that lies under your feet as you explore the higher land around the marsh. About 10 000 years ago, a gigantic lake covered the Edmonton area, its water held in place by huge glaciers. As the glaciers melted, the lake drained away, leaving expanses of muddy sand and silt. Strong winds blew much of this dirt to far off places, but the heavy sand was deposited here, where it is now called the Devon Sandhills. (Pine Knoll Trail)

Look for the tiger beetle scurrying away as you approach. If you get too close, it will suddenly fly up and then land some distance away. As a larva, this predator is ferocious for its size and waits in tiny pits in the sand for its prey to come along. When an insect approaches or falls into the pit, the larva grabs it with powerful jaws. (Meadow Trail, exposed sandy areas)

WILD STRAWBERRIES

FOR MORE INFORMATION, CONTACT:
Alberta Sustainable Resource Development, Fish and Wildlife Division, Stony Plain
Phone: (780) 963-6131

This site is managed by a local volunteer group, the Clifford E. Lee Nature Sanctuary Management Committee, 51306 Rge. Rd. 264, Spruce Grove, Alberta T7Y 1E7

23

Coyote Lake

The Coyote Lake Nature Sanctuary is owned and managed by the Nature Conservancy of Canada (NCC). In 1996, Doris and Eric Hopkins donated their house and wilderness retreat to the NCC. They live on the sanctuary as its stewards and welcome visitors who wish to enjoy the natural wonders of their site, especially the ample birding opportunities. Three ecological zones meet in this area: boreal forest, aspen parkland and foothills. This diverse mix of vegetation attracts over 160 species of birds. Within just a few kilometres of trails, you'll get a wonderful taste of that diversity. Begin by enjoying the views from around the Hopkins' House. A boardwalk takes you over the marshy shoreline to get a full view of the lake.

Special features

Loons nesting on Coyote Lake are in easy view of the main house. The sight of young fluffy loon chicks riding on their parents' backs (June-July) will bring a smile to your face. Visiting loons sometimes join in a social ritual with the nesting pair. With much yodeling, they form a ring, dive into the water, surface about 8 m away and then regroup to repeat their loon square dance. (mornings in June and July for optimum birding on the lake, viewing platforms in first meadow and at end of boardwalk leading from the Hopkins' House)

Great blue herons commonly feed at this lake. They are probably yearlings (hatched the previous summer) from a nearby nesting colony. Yearlings don't nest and are not well tolerated by nesting birds. These immatures must find their own feeding habitat and this lake seems to fill the bill. (early evenings)

The sanctuary supports 22 species of mammals. Moose, deer and wapiti (elk) are attracted to a natural mineral lick at Saltlick Viewpoint. After

LOCATION:
94 km southwest of Edmonton city centre via Leduc

SUGGESTED FIRST-TIME VIEWING:
1 hour to hike to the lake boardwalk and around the first meadow.

ON ARRIVAL:
Proceed to the Hopkins' House to register (at a box) and pick up a map/brochure before parking by the picnic area.

THINGS TO DO:
- ask your resident hosts to set up a spotting scope to get a better view of the lake

COMMON LOON

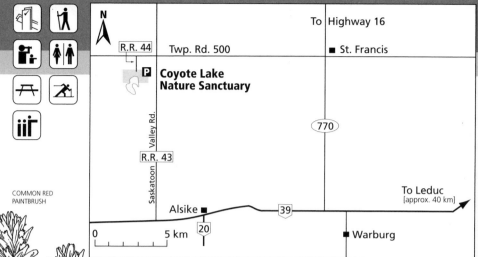

To Highway 16

R.R. 44   Twp. Rd. 500   ■ St. Francis

P   **Coyote Lake**
     Nature Sanctuary

770

Saskatoon Valley Rd.

R.R. 43

To Leduc
[approx. 40 km]

Alsike ■   39

0   5 km   20

■ Warburg

COMMON RED
PAINTBRUSH

passing through some dense bush, the trail opens on a rise overlooking a grassy bowl. Wildlife tracks are everywhere on the wet ground of this scenic and wild place. Make a visit at dawn or dusk for a fine chance of seeing moose, deer or elk. (Saltlick Viewpoint and Moose Meadow)

You'll find wildflowers in each of the many habitats of Coyote Lake. In wet areas, marsh marigolds show their sunny, yellow blooms and cotton grass holds aloft a cottony-white plume. In aspen forest, common red paintbrush and western wood lilies burn fire-red and orange in the undergrowth. The mauve flowers of round-leaved orchids can be seen in low areas among the black spruce. Over 260 species of vascular plants have been identified at the sanctuary, including a number of rare and uncommon orchids.

Stop in during the winter to ski the trails and enjoy the winter birds attracted to the feeders at the Hopkins' House. Blue jays, gray jays, downy and hairy woodpeckers, white-breasted nuthatches and evening grosbeaks are common visitors.

FOR MORE INFORMATION, CONTACT:

Doris and Eric Hopkins, Warburg
Phone: (780) 848-2428

Nature Conservancy of Canada, Alberta Region
Phone: 1-877-262-1253 (toll free)

Web site through Nature Conservancy of Canada: www.natureconservancy.ca

MOOSE

25

Devonian Botanic Garden

[UNIVERSITY OF ALBERTA]

LOCATION:
5 km north of Devon, 33 km southwest of Edmonton city centre via Hwy. 16 and Hwy. 60

SUGGESTED FIRST-TIME VIEWING:
1.5 hours to hike through the tamarack fen

ACCESS RESTRICTIONS:
an admission fee and restricted hours (approximately 10 a.m. to 5 p.m.) in effect from early May to early October. No public access during the winter.

THINGS TO DO:
- tour the Butterfly House and Kurimoto Japanese Garden
- join an event or take a course; programs are offered for all age groups

The Devonian Botanic Garden presents a huge variety of plant species from far and wide, including the "Plants of Alberta" collection and the "Native Peoples' Garden." In addition, a 450-ha natural area is connected to the garden facility and leads you through stands of tamarack, birch, poplar and pine.

Special features

The planted gardens include a good selection of plants you're likely to see in the wilds of Alberta. The difference is—they're all labeled! You'll be able to identify shooting stars, yellow ladies' slippers, bright orange western wood lilies and blue-eyed grass at all stages of their development. Be sure to visit in the fall to see them bearing seeds. They often look like different plants altogether and every bit as fascinating.

In the natural area, a boardwalk takes you to the heart of a tamarack fen. What's so special about the tamarack (also called larch)? It's the only coniferous tree whose needles turn golden in the fall and drop off, leaving the tree bare over the winter months. Look closely and you'll see how the needles grow in clumps on the branch—a useful field mark. Watch for boreal chickadees and hairy woodpeckers probing for insects that live in the rough cracks of the bark. The forest floor displays a lush growth of mosses, the elegant white flowers of buckbean and the spruce-scented wild black currant.

What is a fen? It is peatland or muskeg—a poorly

TAMARACK

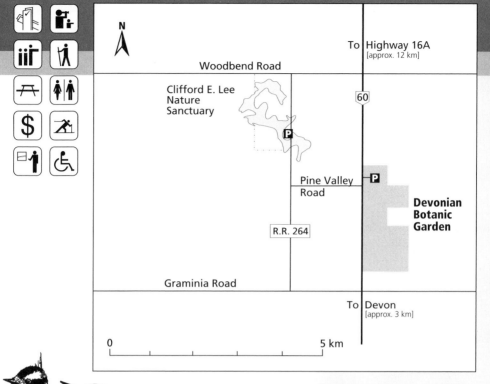

N

To Highway 16A
[approx. 12 km]

Woodbend Road

Clifford E. Lee
Nature
Sanctuary

60

P

Pine Valley
Road

P

**Devonian
Botanic
Garden**

R.R. 264

Graminia Road

To Devon
[approx. 3 km]

0   5 km

DOWNY AND HAIRY WOODPECKERS

drained area where the ground is water-saturated, cool, oxygen-poor and lacking in nutrients. All these characteristics allow a continual build-up of undecomposed plants or peat.

In the tamarack fen and in other wet areas of the site, you'll commonly see horsetail (scouring rush). This unusual plant grows up to a metre in height with slender branches growing from joints along the stem. It produces spores—as do mushrooms—to reproduce itself. More than 300 million years ago, the typical horsetail was a tree, growing to 20 m in height. Coal deposits contain the remains of those ancient forests of horsetail.

SCOURING RUSH

**FOR MORE
INFORMATION, CONTACT:**
Devonian Botanic Garden
Phone: (780) 987-3054
Web: www.discoveredmonton.com/devonian

The Devonian Botanic Garden is operated by the University of Alberta as a research and educational facility.

27

Hasse Lake

LOCATION:
40 km west of Edmonton city centre

SUGGESTED FIRST-TIME VIEWING:
1 hour to walk the 3-km loop trail

THINGS TO DO:
- cast a line from the dock or lakeshore to catch some of the stocked rainbow trout.
- ice-fishing is popular at this lake.

At this County of Parkland day use area, you can enjoy a 3-km walk along the trails combined with a few casts of your fishing line. An enclosed picnic shelter is just the thing to cook up your catch over a crackling fire. Bring some wieners just in case the fish aren't biting! The poplar forest has a dense undergrowth of beaked hazelnut, red-osier dogwood and prickly rose. Around the lake, wet-loving willows and cattails protect nesting birds. Sit quietly along the lakeshore and take in the sights and sounds.

Special features

The 6-cm brook stickleback is a fish named for the five or six spines on its back. The male is a conscientious parent, building a nest out of plant stems and defending the eggs until they are hatched. The threespine stickleback was illegally introduced to the lake and first noticed in 1980. This invader now competes with native fish and greatly outnumbers the brook stickleback. Get the kids to catch one of these prickly little fish to identify. Be careful not to get jabbed and be sure to return it after getting a close look. It is very important not to transfer any aquatic plants or animals to other water bodies where they may cause unintended harm. (Sticklebacks are best seen in spring when spawning adjacent the floating dock.)

The poplar forest at Hasse Lake is particularly rich in woodland birds. Ruffed grouse spend their time on the ground and in the trees searching out buds, seeds and insects to feed on. In the spring, the male attracts a mate by rapidly beating his wings. He sounds like a muffled lawn mower starting up. Yellow warblers, sometimes called wild canaries, can be seen flitting through the trees. White-throated sparrows regularly sing from

RUFFED GROUSE

28

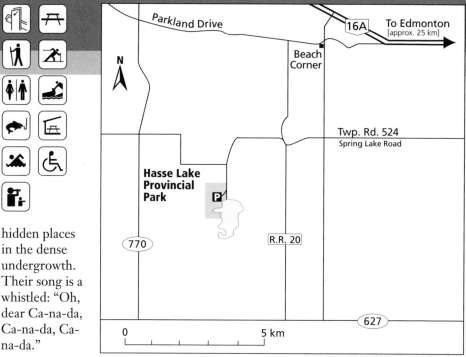

Parkland Drive

To Edmonton
[approx. 25 km]
16A

Beach
Corner

N

Twp. Rd. 524
Spring Lake Road

Hasse Lake
Provincial
Park

P

770

R.R. 20

627

0   5 km

hidden places in the dense undergrowth. Their song is a whistled: "Oh, dear Ca-na-da, Ca-na-da, Ca-na-da."

On the lake, the ruddy duck males are the clowns of the waterfowl family with their blue bills, white cheeks and stubby upright tails. As they court the females, they chuck their heads backward and forward and make a sputtering sound with their bills. American coots, when alarmed, will usually patter along the surface to get away, rather than taking to the air. Notice how coots bob their heads back and forth, like a chicken, as they swim. That behaviour has earned them the name "mudhen."

RUDDY DUCK

As you walk by open areas along the trails, you'll see little mounds of earth that show no openings. After spring cleaning, the mound-makers plug up the entrance holes to discourage intruders. These mounds indicate burrows that belong to the northern pocket gopher, often mistakenly called a "mole." (In fact, there are no moles in Alberta.) Like a mole, however, the pocket gopher is rarely seen. It tunnels down as much as 3 m below the surface, collecting roots to store for winter. Normally, it feeds on green plant material only when it comes to the surface at night.

FOR MORE INFORMATION, CONTACT:
The County of Parkland, Recreation and Park Services
Phone: (780) 968-8888
Web: www.parklandcounty. com/tourism

Alberta Sustainable Resource Development's *Fishing in Alberta* web site:
www3.gov.ab.ca/srd/fw/ fishing/

29

Matchayaw (Devil's) Lake

LOCATION:
46 km west of Edmonton city centre

SUGGESTED FIRST-TIME VIEWING:
2 hours at Imrie Park to view waterfowl at the blind and explore some of the trails.

THINGS TO DO:

- in Imrie Park, hike the Branting Trail east to the Watchable Wildlife Blind on the west shore of the lake. Take your binoculars and camera.

- in winter, ski the many trails in Imrie Park and look for tracks of red squirrel, ermine, coyote and spruce grouse in the snow.

- visit the nearby Bilby Natural Area.

Matchayaw Lake (locally know as Devil's Lake) is 2 km long and 1 km wide, with a maximum depth of about 10 metres. Along its west shore, large tracts of shallow water and associated wetlands, provide prime feeding and nesting areas for waterfowl. The best place to view the waterfowl and other wildlife is through Imrie Park on the west shore of the lake.

Special features

Mallards, scaups, green-winged teal, northern shovelers, Canada geese and other waterfowl come to this lake in the spring to breed or rest on their way further north. Mating rituals and territorial displays are just some of the interesting behaviour that can be observed. Later in the spring and summer, families of birds, such as the red-necked grebe, are seen feeding in the shallows or diving in the deep.

In 1988, Edmonton architect Mary Louise Imrie (1918-88) bequeathed the land for Imrie Park to the Province of Alberta through the Alberta Sport, Recreation, Parks and Wildlife Foundation "for conservation and public enjoyment." The foundation worked with the people of Onoway and area to plan and develop the park, largely through the volunteer efforts of the Onoway Fish and Game Club. The club manages the 87-hectare park, which includes a

NORTHERN SHOVELER

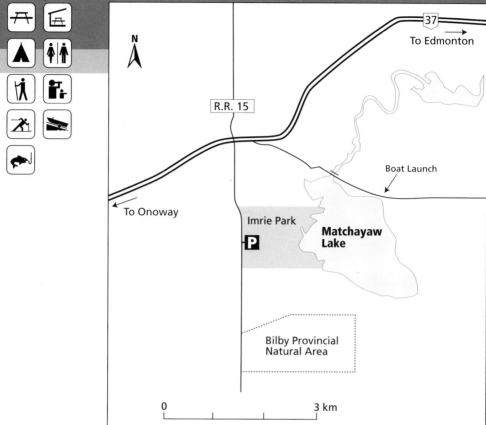

campground and kitchen shelters. A system of well maintained hiking and cross-country ski trails takes you through a variety of wildlife habitats, including black spruce muskeg, tamarack, aspen and jack pine forests.

The focal point for wildlife watching in the park is the Watchable Wildlife Blind on the shore of Matchayaw Lake. This structure, built of rough-hewn timber, is ideal for unobtrusively observing waterfowl and other wildlife on the lake. It will comfortably hold 12 or more people at one time, and displays posters and signs to aid in wildlife identification. The blind is situated so that quiet observers can easily enter and leave it without disturbing the wildlife on the lake.

FOR MORE INFORMATION, CONTACT:
Alberta Sport, Recreation, Parks and Wildlife Foundation
Phone: (780) 415-0266
Web: through
www.cd.gov.ab.ca/asrpwf/

31

St. Albert – Sturgeon River

LOCATION:
14 km northwest of Edmonton city centre on St. Albert Trail

SUGGESTED FIRST-TIME VIEWING:
1.5 hours to walk Big Lake Interpretive Trail; 1 hour to walk the short self-guiding trail at Red Willow Park; and 2 hours to walk the trails at River Lot 56.

THINGS TO DO:
- pick up a self-guiding trail guide at St. Albert Place. The trail has no stop markers, so follow directions carefully

GETTING THERE:
Most of the above sites may be reached using the Red Willow Trail system. Pick up a complete map at St. Albert Place. The Big Lake Interpretive Trail is reached via Meadowview Drive (see Big Lake – Matchayaw Lake Auto Tour, page 62).

SUGGESTED READINGS FOR MORE DISCOVERY:
Natural History Walking Tour (booklet). 1992. Musée Héritage Museum, St. Albert Place, St. Albert, Alberta.

The City of St. Albert is blessed with a variety of natural areas within and adjacent to the community. Red Willow Park links many of these areas through a strip of green along the Sturgeon River. In the southwest, Big Lake attracts thousands of birds during spring and fall migrations. River Lot 56, in the northeast, is a designated natural area with 16 km of trails winding through poplar woodland and meadow.

Special features

Big Lake
This 10-km by 2-km shallow body of water is almost separated into two parts by a delta formed from an accumulation of soil carried in by the Sturgeon River. The lake has been designated a Natural Area under the Special Places 2000 program, and is an internationally recognized Important Bird Area (www.ibacanada.com) because of its significance as a migratory stopping place for tundra swans and nesting area for Franklin's gull. Waterfowl begin arriving by mid-March and include Canada geese and tundra swans. Northern pintails are among the first ducks. These graceful birds with slender necks and long tails migrate from California or the Gulf of Mexico. Notice how they are often already paired by the time they arrive at Big Lake.

One of the best places to view bird life is along the Big Lake Interpretive Trail established by Ducks Unlimited and the Rotary Club of St. Albert in 1996. Take Meadow View Drive from the southwest corner of St. Albert and drive 7.2 km from the railroad track crossing to the start of the trail marked by the Ducks Unlimited sign. Park at the designated space and walk the trail leading toward the lake. Interpretive signs help you identify wildlife along the way.

Red Willow Park
Explore some of the 40 km of trails along the Sturgeon River for a good view of wildlife in a

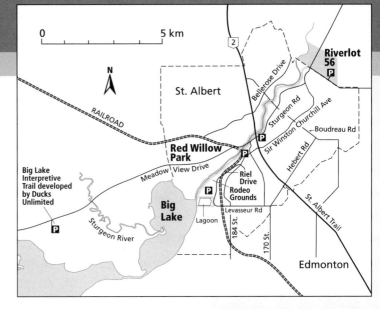

riparian environment. A 2-km self-guiding trail takes you from the train trestle, dating from the early days of settlement, through the natural vegetation along the river. Cinnamon teal can be seen on the river. The younger members of your group may spot, in wet areas, tiger salamanders (you can't mistake its blotchy patterns) and wood frogs (with a black mask and white jaw stripe). A viewing platform at the NW corner of the lagoon where the river leaves Big Lake provides a good view of the river.

River Lot 56

Follow the change of wildflowers through the seasons at this provincial natural area. In spring, poplar and willow catkins release their white, fluffy seeds, which cover trail edges like a dusting of snow. During summer, bees gather nectar from the bright yellow goldenrod blooms. Saskatoon, raspberry, choke cherry and pin cherry burst with a crop of juicy berries. In the fall, look for the plump, white berries of the snowberry shrubs and delicate berries of star-flowered Solomon's-seal (neither are good to eat). September brings a blissfully peaceful scene as the sun shines through leaves painted yellow, orange and red. In winter, the woods become even more peaceful as bright red branches of red-osier dogwood and frozen red rosehips decorate the undergrowth above a blanket of snow.

RED-OSIER DOGWOOD

FOR MORE INFORMATION, CONTACT:

City of St. Albert
Phone: (780) 459-1500
Web: www.city.st-albert.ab.ca

BLESS (Big Lake Environment Support Society)
Box 65053, St. Albert Centre
St. Albert, Alberta, T8N 5Y3
Web: www.bless.ab.ca

33

Wabamun Lake

LOCATION:

65 km west of Edmonton city centre

SUGGESTED FIRST-TIME VIEWING:

1.5 hours to explore the shoreline adjacent the day use area at Wabamun Lake Provincial Park

THINGS TO DO:

- participate in the Wabamun Christmas Bird Count
- spend the weekend camped at the Provincial Park

Wabamun Lake is long (20 km), shallow (averages 6.5 m), and is rich in nutrients, so it produces an abundant crop of aquatic weeds, invertebrates and fish. Fish-eating birds find this a terrific place to raise their young. The warm water flushed into the lake from the Wabamun power plant keeps a section of the lake ice-free during winter, encouraging many birds to stay year-round. You can get good views of the lake from the wharf at the town of Wabamun, from Wabamun Lake Provincial Park or from the south side of the lake at Goosequill Bay.

Special features

The osprey is a fish hawk that cruises over the shallows looking for fish swimming near the surface. When it spots a fish, it dives straight into the water, sometimes disappearing from sight and, if successful, emerges with a fish in its talons. Ospreys nest in large stick nests high in the trees or on power poles around the lake.

Common terns have a similar hunting style for catching minnows. After the young learn to fly, they can be seen chasing after the parents and begging for a meal.

The belted kingfisher sits on branches overlooking the shoreline and waits for prey to appear. Fish, frogs and large insects are favourite foods. Listen for the loud rattling call, often made in flight.

OSPREY

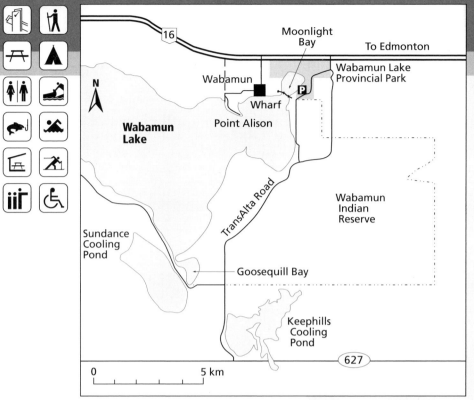

16

Moonlight
Bay

To Edmonton

Wabamun Lake
Provincial Park

Wabamun

P

Wharf

Point Alison

N

**Wabamun
Lake**

TransAlta Road

Wabamun
Indian
Reserve

Sundance
Cooling
Pond

Goosequill Bay

Keephills
Cooling
Pond

627

0   5 km

The great blue heron relies on stealth, and patience, standing frozen in the shallows of the lake waiting for prey to come within range. With a sudden thrust and jab, the heron spears itself a meal. (reedy shorelines)

WHITE SUCKER

Fish-eating birds prey on pike, perch and white suckers. In spring, watch for these fish spawning (laying eggs) in the shallow water and in streams entering the lake. Whitefish are particularly noticeable during the fall, spawning in the shallows by the railway trestle where Moonlight Bay joins the main lake. (Oct.-Nov.)

Winter birdwatching may reward you with a sighting of a bald eagle or a gyrfalcon searching for a meal among the overwintering mallards and common goldeneyes. Gyrfalcons overwinter at Wabamun Lake before heading back to the Arctic to nest.

**FOR MORE
INFORMATION, CONTACT:**
Wabamun Lake Provincial Park,
Park Office
Phone: (780) 892-2702
Web: through
www.cd.gov.ab.ca/
enjoying_alberta/parks/

35

Wagner Natural Area

LOCATION:
22 km west of Edmonton city centre on Hwy. 16

SUGGESTED FIRST-TIME VIEWING:
1.5 hours to walk the self-guiding trail

THINGS TO DO:
- join a "Toad Walk" in spring or attend other special events
- wear boots and insect repellent during warm and wet seasons
- stay on the trails since wetlands are very sensitive to trampling

SUGGESTED READINGS FOR MORE DISCOVERY:
Marl Pond Trail, self-guiding trail booklet, by members of the Wagner Natural Area Society.

Take your time as you walk this site's short trail (1.2 km) and explore a natural area packed with fascinating sights, including some very special wild orchids and carnivorous plants. A looped trail and boardwalk take you past soggy fens, marl ponds, willow swamp and muskeg forest of spruce and tamarack.

Special features

Do some plants really eat animals? You bet they do! See if you can spot these seldom-noticed carnivorous plants. They digest insects to gain a nitrogen supplement.

The round-leaved sundew occurs on hummocks of sphagnum moss. When the spoon-shaped leaves with their sticky red hairs trap an insect, they fold over and slowly digest it. Watch for yourself! (flowers July)

Butterworts trap insects in much the same way. The purple flowers resemble a violet and you'll find them growing on the edge of the marl ponds. (flowers June-July)

Bladderworts, which grow in shallow water, extend long stems above the surface to show off bright yellow blooms in July. Attached to the underwater leaves, little bladders open suddenly when stimulated by tiny aquatic animals. The prey is quickly sucked in, where it dies and gives the plant nourishment as the prey decays.

Watching toads and frogs is a great family activity. In early May, look for a twin-strand necklace of "black beads" covered in grey jelly (toad eggs) or dark spots in a round mass of jelly (wood frog eggs). In warm weather, the eggs soon hatch into tadpoles: greenish brown tadpoles

WOOD FROG

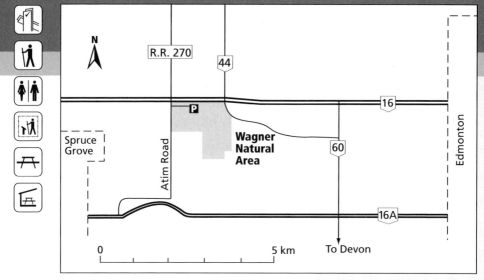

R.R. 270 | 44

P

16

Spruce Grove

Atim Road

Wagner Natural Area

60

Edmonton

16A

0   5 km   To Devon

N

SHOOTING STAR

are wood frogs; black tadpoles are boreal toads. On spring evenings, listen to the bird-like trill of the male toads calling to the females.

Marl ponds are fed by groundwater springs that are very rich in calcium carbonate, the same white crust that forms around bathroom faucets. When the calcium carbonate settles out, it mixes with peat—dead plants that haven't decomposed in the waterlogged soil—to form the whitish paste called marl. Stonewort is an aptly named common plant of the ponds that becomes encrusted with marl and is rough to the touch. Also, look for a curly brown moss growing at the edge of the ponds, named "fen pasta" by local students.

Marsh marigolds are among the first flowers to bloom in the spring: big, bright and yellow. They are followed by large blue bog violets and pink, pointed shooting stars. In summer, western wood lilies, slender white asters and blue-fringed gentians show their blooms. Mauve flowers of the round-leaved orchid appear abundantly in the spruce woods at the north end of the trail in June. It is one of 16 orchid species found at this site.

FOR MORE INFORMATION, CONTACT:
Wagner Natural Area Society
Mail: 26519 Highway 16,
Spruce Grove, Alberta T7X 3L4
Phone: (780) 427-8124
Web: http://wagner.fanweb.ca

The Wagner Natural Area Society is the volunteer steward for the site under the Natural Areas Program. It leases and manages the site for conservation purposes and nature education.

37

East
of Edmonton

[VIEWING SITES]

SITE NAME	DISTANCE FROM EDMONTON CITY CENTRE	SPECIAL FEATURES	PAGE
1 Beaverhill Lake (Tofield)	67 km E	prime location for watching migrating birds: geese, swans, ducks, shorebirds, bald eagles, hawks, falcons	40
2 Blackfoot Recreation Area	47 km E	150 km of trails, great blue herons, wapiti, moose, deer, beaver, northern orioles, yellow warblers, double-crested cormorants, American white pelicans	42
3 Dow Wildlife Greenbelt Viewing Area	35 km NE	Richardson's ground squirrels, Swainson's hawks, nesting waterfowl, common goldeneyes, killdeers, ring-necked pheasants	44
4 Elk Island National Park	47 km E	103 km of trails, Beaver Hills, high concentration of hoofed mammals: wood bison, wapiti, moose, white-tailed deer	46
5 Halfmoon Lake Natural Area	54 km N	sandhills, jack pine, bog cranberry, bearberry, reindeer lichen, common nighthawks, cedar waxwings, historic Athabasca Landing	48
6 Miquelon Lake Provincial Park	70 km SE	beaver, red-necked grebes, aspen, western plains garter snakes, American avocets, snowshoe hares	50
7 Sherwood Park Natural Area	18 km E	great-horned owls, northern saw-whet owls, pileated woodpeckers, wood frogs, boreal chorus frogs, flowering shrubs, Old Edmonton Trail	52
8 Strathcona Wilderness Centre	34 km E	black spruce bog, porcupines, red squirrels, red-breasted nuthatches, Labrador tea, sphagnum moss, old man's beard	54
9 Telford Lake (Leduc)	35 km S	cattails, red-winged blackbirds, marsh wrens, water fleas, migrating ducks and geese, mallards	56

38

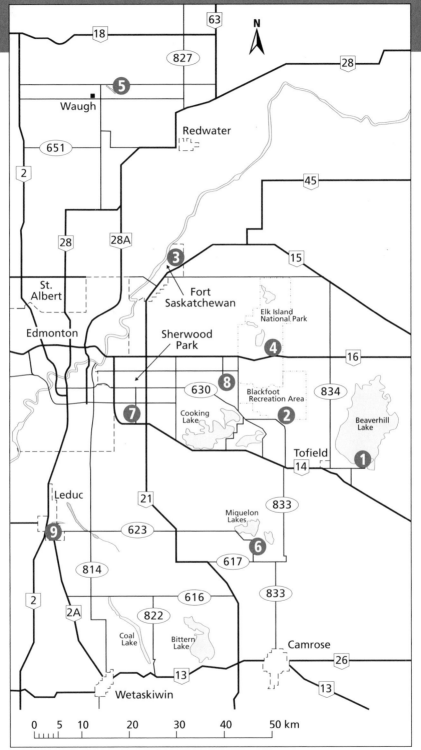

N

18
63
827
5
Waugh
28
651
2
28
28A
3
Fort
Saskatchewan
45
15
St.
Albert
Elk Island
National Park
Edmonton
Sherwood
Park
4
16
630
8
Blackfoot
Recreation Area
834
7
Cooking
Lake
2
Beaverhill
Lake
Tofield
1
14
21
Leduc
833
Miquelon
Lakes
623
9
6
617
814
833
2
616
2A
822
Coal
Lake
Bittern
Lake
Camrose
26
13
13
Wetaskiwin

0 5 10   20   30   40   50 km

Beaverhill Lake

[TOFIELD]

LOCATION:
67 km east of Edmonton city centre on Hwy. 14

SUGGESTED FIRST-TIME VIEWING:
1 hour to explore Francis Viewpoint and the bird blind, 3 hours to hike the natural area trails.

THINGS TO DO:

- watch the bird-banding activities in spring or summer at the Beaverhill Bird Observatory
- attend the Snow Goose Festival held during the third weekend in April and the Fall Migration Celebrations on the fourth weekend of September

FOR SUCCESSFUL VIEWING:

- stop in at the Beaverhill Lake Nature Centre
- bring warm clothing and rubber boots since this site can be windy, cold and wet
- bring binoculars and spotting scopes to identify birds at a distance
- caution: roads can be very slippery when wet

Imagine looking out over a seemingly endless expanse of water when suddenly wave upon wave of snow geese fly in formation overhead. Beaverhill Lake is a Ramsar site—internationally recognized as a special place for migrating birds. It is a gigantic prairie slough (10 km x 20 km) with inflow during wet periods and outflow only during high water years.

Special features

Beaverhill is the place to see spectacular numbers of migrating waterfowl and shorebirds. In spring, these birds head as far north as the High Arctic to breed. In fall, when they make the return trip, they fly to the southern United States and even as far as South America.

Listen to geese honking loudly as they fly overhead or rest in the shallow water along the shore. Locally breeding Canada geese are the first to arrive—as early as March 1. Over the next 6-10 weeks Canada, snow, Ross' and greater white-fronted geese arrive in waves. Thousands can be seen on any given day during the peak of migration. They rest overnight at the lake and, from about mid-morning till early evening, feed in nearby sloughs and fields.

The more common of our two swan species is the tundra swan. It nests in the far north and overwinters in the United States, passing Beaverhill on its way to and fro. Watch for these elegant all-white birds, which feed in shallow water near the shore. The best time to see them is in the fall when some stay until the lake freezes.

Sandhill cranes give a distinctive musical rattle as they fly overhead during late April to early May in kilometre-long

CANADA GOOSE

40

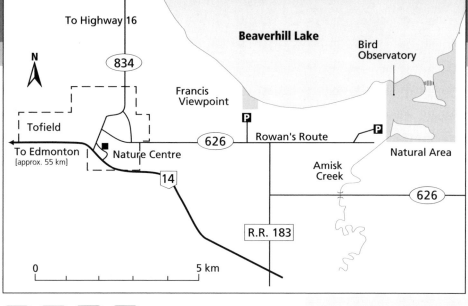

Map labels:
To Highway 16
N
834
Beaverhill Lake
Bird Observatory
Francis Viewpoint
Tofield
P
To Edmonton [approx. 55 km]
Nature Centre
626
Rowan's Route
P
Natural Area
14
Amisk Creek
R.R. 183
626
0   5 km

flocks. They nest in central and northern Alberta, as well as farther north.

Shorebirds such as the killdeer (local nesters) and dowitchers (mostly northern nesters) are attracted to the extensive mudflats and rocky shorelines around the lake. Over 20 000 shorebirds stop at the lake each year, with numbers peaking around mid-May and again in mid-August.

Bald eagles migrate past the lake in spring and fall, often stopping to scavenge dead birds frozen in the ice. Spring is the best time to see up to 18 species of hawks and falcons.

SHOREBIRDS

SUGGESTED READINGS FOR MORE DISCOVERY:
Prairie Water: Watchable Wildlife at Beaverhill Lake, Alberta. 1991. Dick Dekker, BST Publications, Edmonton, Alberta.

FOR MORE INFORMATION, CONTACT:
Beaverhill Lake Nature Centre, Tofield
Phone: (780) 662-3191
Web: www.tofieldalberta.ca/nature.htm

Tofield Town Office:
Phone: (780) 662-3269

or

Beaverhill Bird Observatory
Mail: Box 1418, Edmonton T5J 2N5

Birds of Beaverhill Lake web site: www.connect.ab.ca/~snowyowl/index.htm

Blackfoot

Hike into the interior of Blackfoot and you quickly forget how close you are to a large city. With over 150 km of trails winding through 97 km² of rolling landscape, mostly covered with broadleaf forests and meadows, get set for a real backcountry experience.

Many different users cooperate to make Blackfoot Recreation Area a success. Industrial and agricultural uses (natural gas extraction and cattle grazing) take place alongside hunting, trapping and recreational activities (hiking, horseback-riding, skiing).

Special features

Blackfoot Staging Area

Many great blue herons nest in a colony on Blackfoot Lake. The large stick nests sit high in poplar trees and are most noticeable when the leaves are off the trees. During the breeding season (April 15 to July 30), please keep at least 200 m away from the nest colony. (Whitetail Trail)

Blackfoot has enough territory for significant populations of wapiti (elk), moose and deer. Listen for bugling male wapiti challenging each other in the early fall. Look for aspen saplings rubbed by the males of deer, wapiti and moose as they polish their antlers for the fall rut. (Buckrun Trail)

Central Staging Area

Well-worn beaver runs, leading to water, are common around lakes in the area. Each active beaver lodge on a lake may house the parents, two or three young from the previous year and the new kits born in spring. (Beaver Trail)

LOCATION:
47 km east of Edmonton city centre

SUGGESTED FIRST-TIME VIEWING:
1 hour to walk the Neon Lake Trail and return by way of Lost Lake Trail (Waskehegan Staging Area)

THINGS TO DO:
- ride a mountain bike or hike into the secluded interior
- plan a picnic at one of the backcountry shelters
- launch a canoe at the boat ramp on Islet Lake
- cross-country ski

FOR SUCCESSFUL VIEWING:
- pick up a map at any staging area and bring a compass to keep you on the right track

WAPITI (ELK)

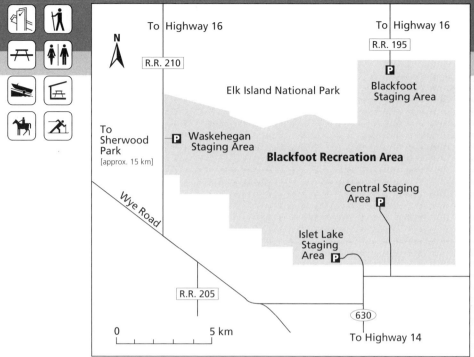

To Highway 16

R.R. 210

N

To Highway 16

R.R. 195

P

Blackfoot
Staging Area

Elk Island National Park

To
Sherwood
Park
[approx. 15 km]

P Waskehegan
Staging Area

Blackfoot Recreation Area

Central Staging
Area P

Islet Lake
Staging
Area P

Wye Road

R.R. 205

630

0   5 km

To Highway 14

Birds of the forest make colourful and musical companions. Watch for the northern oriole and yellow warbler as they search for insects in the upper branches of the aspen trees.

GREAT BLUE HERON

Waskehegan Staging Area
Spruce Hollow Trail takes you through a spruce grove that survived a fire that burned through this area in the early 1900s. Spruce forests are shady and cool in the summer. Lean against a tree and savour the peaceful mood. Look among the spruce needles and feather mosses of the ground carpet for bunchberry, twinflower, horsetail and wintergreen.

Islet Lake Staging Area
The interior lakes of Blackfoot offer secluded places for water birds to rest during migration or to nest for the summer. To get a good view of the water, take Lost Lake and Push Lake trails, which follow a ridge around Islet Lake. Look for double-crested cormorants and American white pelicans.

FOR MORE INFORMATION, CONTACT:
Blackfoot Recreation Area Office
Phone: (780) 922-3293
Web: www.edmontonplus.ca/profile/34851/

Information Line:
Phone: (780) 922-4676

43

Dow Wildlife Greenbelt

[VIEWING AREA]

Can wildlife habitat function successfully alongside an industrial site? Come see for yourself. Dow Chemical is making a concerted effort with the development of a greenbelt around its Hydrocarbon Plant. The 8-ha greenbelt reduces the plant's impact by providing habitat for wildlife to raise their young and to use as a movement corridor. At the viewing area, red shale paths lead you across a meadow to a raised platform overlooking marsh and pond.

Special features

Richardson's ground squirrels are Alberta's best known "gopher." Listen for their warning whistles when you get too close, then watch them go scampering down their burrows. They have many different exits to make good their escape, if a weasel should decide to follow them.

Watch for a Swainson's or red-tailed hawk sitting on a power pole nearby. These common hawks of open areas will swoop down for a meal of ground squirrel, mouse or even grasshopper.

The open waters of specially designed ponds at the public viewing site are fine places to see nesting waterfowl. Nesting islands constructed in the ponds provide safe nesting habitat for shorebirds, ducks and geese. Nesting boxes are placed in trees near the pond for common goldeneye. These ducks normally nest in abandoned woodpecker holes. It's amazing how small a cavity can accommodate this duck and its young. After hatching, the young tumble out and follow the female, to be raised among the reeds of the pond.

A common shorebird, the killdeer, shrieks frantically and feigns injury to distract

KILLDEER

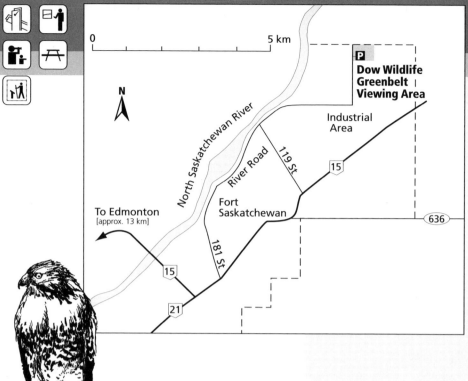

0   5 km

N

North Saskatchewan River

River Road

119 St

15

P
Dow Wildlife Greenbelt Viewing Area

Industrial Area

To Edmonton
[approx. 13 km]

Fort Saskatchewan

181 St

15

21

636

RED-TAILED HAWK

you from finding its nest or young. The eggs are laid right in the open, on the ground. They are so well camouflaged that one usually finds them only by accident. Hours after hatching, the young begin following their parents, learning to hunt insects.

Ring-necked pheasants are native to southern China and were first introduced into Alberta in 1908. The local fish and game club released them in the greenbelt where fields of sweet clover, blue flax and alfalfa provide food and cover for nesting. The most difficult part of their existence is surviving our winters.

RED FOX

FOR MORE INFORMATION, CONTACT:
Dow Chemical Canada Inc.
Web: www.dow.com/facilities/namerica/canada/ehs/ehs02.htm

Fort Saskatchewan
Web: www.fortsask.ca

45

Elk Island

LOCATION:

47 km east of Edmonton city centre

SUGGESTED FIRST-TIME VIEWING:

1 to 3 hours to view wildlife along the main road through the park

THINGS TO DO:

- visit the Astotin Interpretive Centre (phone ahead for open hours)
- pond dip for mini-beasts at the Living Waters Boardwalk Trail
- drive the 19-km Elk Island Parkway, the Bison Paddock (May–Sept.), and auxiliary roads

SUGGESTED READINGS FOR MORE DISCOVERY:

The Discoverer's Guide to Elk Island National Park. 1991. Ross Chapman.

Finding Birds in Elk Island National Park. 1988. J. Cornish.

Both of these publications are available from the Friends of Elk Island Society and at the park's Information Centre.

Elk Island is part of the Beaver Hills, a rolling landscape probably named for its large population of beaver so valued during the fur trade era. The diversity of habitat seen along 103 km of trails attracts a year-round parade of birds including pelicans and trumpeter swans. However, more than anything else, you should come here to see moose, deer, wapiti (elk) and bison—representing some of the highest big game densities in North America.

Special features

Elk Island has one of the highest concentrations of hoofed mammals in the world.

The wood bison is North America's largest native land mammal, weighing up to 1200 kg. In the mid-1960s, one of only two remaining North American herds of wood bison was transferred to the park. Today, under careful management, the species is no longer considered endangered; however, it is still listed as threatened. Watch the bison graze in the open meadows year-round. In the spring, rust-coloured calves frolic around their shaggy parents. Look for wood bison in the area on the south side of Highway 16 and plains bison on the north side. Keep your distance from these animals—bison are dangerous. (Hayburger Trail, Mud Lake Corral fences at Tawayik Lake Trail, Wood Bison Trail, Bison Paddock, parkway)

The park was originally established to protect 24 wapiti (elk) remaining in the area. Today, this species is the most common large mammal in the park. In the fall, listen for the shrill bugling of the bulls, during early morning or

RED-NECKED GREBE

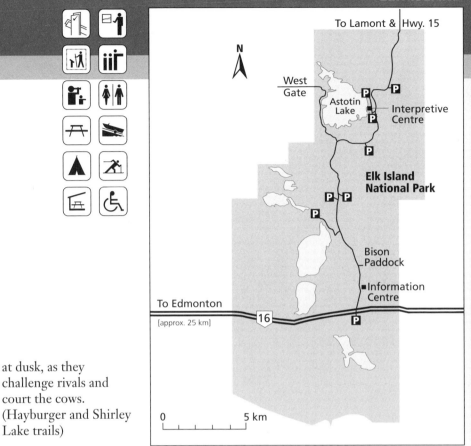

To Lamont & Hwy. 15

N

West
Gate

Astotin
Lake

P P

P Interpretive
Centre

P

Elk Island
National Park

P P

P

Bison
Paddock

Information
Centre

To Edmonton
[approx. 25 km]

16

P

0   5 km

at dusk, as they challenge rivals and court the cows. (Hayburger and Shirley Lake trails)

Moose and white-tailed deer browse along the edges of shrubby or forested areas. Winter is a great time to see them contrasted against the white snow and exposed among the leafless trees. Watch for signs of their activity: cloven-hoofed tracks, chewed shrubs, droppings, packed-down grasses and telltale hairs left behind. (Moss Lake Trail, parkway)

COYOTE

FOR MORE INFORMATION, CONTACT:

Elk Island National Park is administered by Parks Canada

Information Centre
Phone: (780) 992-5790
(summer only)
Web: www.parkscanada.gc.ca/

Interpretation Programs
Phone: (780) 992-6392

Administration:
Phone: (780) 992-6380

Friends of Elk Island Society
Site 4, RR #1
Fort Saskatchewan, AB
T8L 2N7
Web:www.elkisland.ca

47

Halfmoon Lake

LOCATION:
54 km north of Edmonton city centre

SUGGESTED FIRST-TIME VIEWING:
2 hours to hike to the lake and back

THINGS TO DO:
- stay on established trails when exploring this sensitive environment; vegetation is easily disturbed in sandy terrain

Halfmoon Lake Natural Area overlies rolling sandhills next to the shore of Halfmoon Lake. A trail takes you through open pine forests and dense poplar woods, over grassy meadows, and down into areas of wet muskeg and black spruce. Although the trail to the lake is signed, it is not well-traveled and is somewhat rough.

Special features

Jack pine was considered a bad omen by early settlers because it signified dry, sandy soils where crops tended to fail. It's one of the first trees to sprout after a fire. In fact, the cones don't normally open to expose their winged seeds until they have been scorched. In the undergrowth, look for bog cranberry, bearberry (named kinnikinnick by Natives) and reindeer lichen.

Some of the jack pines have dwarf mistletoe growing on their branches. This parasitic flowering plant causes the pine to develop an abnormal cluster of branches called witches' brooms. The fruits of the mistletoe expel seeds to a distance of 10 m. If the seeds lodge in the bark of a tree, a new parasite plant can germinate.

Beginning at dusk, the common nighthawk flies aerobatically over the meadows and open pine forest to snap up insects in its large mouth. It's worth an evening trip just to listen to and, on a clear night, to view this bird dive-bombing for insects. Each dive ends with a miniature sonic boom as the nighthawk suddenly sweeps upward.

Cedar waxwings start nesting in July, later than most birds, because the

JACK PINE

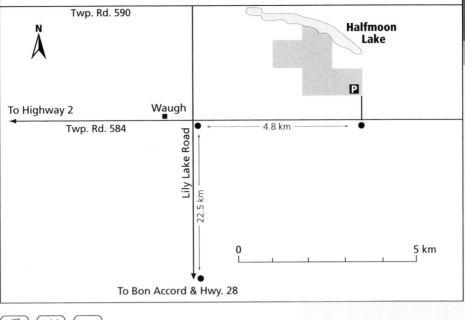

Twp. Rd. 590

N

To Highway 2

Waugh

Twp. Rd. 584

Lily Lake Road

Halfmoon Lake

P

4.8 km

22.5 km

0   5 km

To Bon Accord & Hwy. 28

timing must match the development of their food crop—berries. Look for these birds sitting in a row on a wire, gathering in the crown of a tree or feeding in berry bushes. Berry-producing plants flourish at Halfmoon Lake. You'll find saskatoons, blueberries, raspberries and strawberries. (July–September)

Athabasca Landing Trail is located near the natural area. For information on exploring the trail, go to St. Mary's Church in the village of Waugh. In the late 1800s, missionaries, prospectors and others travelled this route. It connected Fort Edmonton, located along the North Saskatchewan River, with the Athabasca River. During the Klondike Gold Rush, it became Alberta's first Dominion Highway.

BLUEBERRIES

FOR MORE INFORMATION, CONTACT:
Alberta Community Development, Parks and Protected Areas
Phone (toll free):
1-866-427-3582
Web: through www.cd.gov.ab.ca/ enjoying_alberta/parks

49

Miquelon Lake

[PROVINCIAL PARK]

LOCATION:
70 km southeast of
Edmonton city centre

**SUGGESTED
FIRST-TIME VIEWING:**
1/2 hour to walk Grebe Pond
Trail and 1.5 hours to hike
the first loop of the Knob
and Kettle trails

THINGS TO DO:
- drop by the Visitor Centre
  for wildlife displays and
  activity packs to help you
  explore for birds, animal
  tracks and pond life
- attend an interpretive
  program during the
  summer months
- rent a paddleboat to
  navigate the shoreline
- bring the gang out to look
  for active winter wildlife
- after a winter outing,
  stoke a fire in one of the
  enclosed shelters and
  serve up a snack and hot
  drink

**SUGGESTED READINGS
FOR MORE DISCOVERY:**
Summer newspaper and
Discovery book (for children
and families), Miquelon Lake
Provincial Park.

Miquelon roadways and trails are great places for
families to explore for wildlife, particularly during
fall, winter and spring when visitor use is low.
This park is at the southern end and highest point
of the Beaver Hills. As you walk the trails away
from the main lake, the ground rises in elevation
until you're standing high on a forested ridge
overlooking kettle ponds on either side. Walk
further and you come to the second of the three
Miquelon Lakes.

Special features

As you drive into the park, you'll see Grebe Pond
just past the permit booth, on the right side of the
road. Park your vehicle in the parking lot a little
farther on, and follow the shoreline trail.

Beaver have built an impressive lodge in the
middle of Grebe Pond. The best time to see
active beaver is early morning or late evening. The
kids will get a kick out of hearing the "kerplunk"
of a beaver tail as other beaver are warned of your
presence.

Red-necked grebes are easy to spot as they dive for
fish and insects in the open water. With a sharp
eye, you might also spot their floating nests
anchored to reeds along the shoreline. (Grebe
Pond)

The Knob and Kettle Trail system begins at the
baseball diamond. You can hike an easy 2.5-km
loop or go for the whole 8 km, all the way to the
second Miquelon Lake.

Mature aspens line the trails. Take a close look at
this tree's leaf stalks. They're flat like an elastic
band, causing the leaf to tremble in the slightest
breeze. An old aspen forest has many dead trees,
some standing
and some
toppled,

GARTER SNAKE

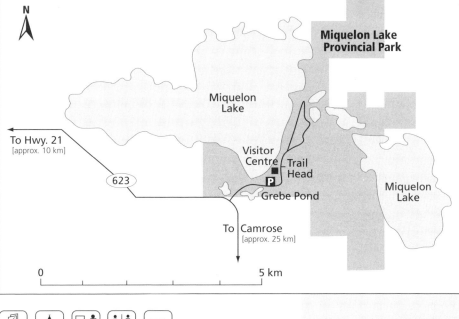

which provide valuable habitats. Woodpeckers use them for building nesting cavities, beetles tunnel in the bark and hares scrape out dens underneath the fallen trees.

Western plains garter snakes like to sun themselves along trail edges and search for insects and small frogs around ponds. Since their skin doesn't stretch, they shed it, usually in one piece, at regular intervals of growth.

Snowshoe hares make their presence very obvious in winter, leaving tracks, browsed shrubs and droppings throughout the wooded areas. Yet their fur blends in beautifully with their surroundings, by being white in winter and grey-brown in summer.

SNOWSHOE HARE

FOR MORE INFORMATION, CONTACT:
Alberta Community Development, Parks and Protected Areas
Phone (toll free):
1-866-427-3582
Web: www.cd.gov.ab.ca/ enjoying_alberta/parks/

Miquelon Park Management Corporation
Phone: (780) 672-7274

51

Sherwood Park

[NATURAL AREA]

LOCATION:
18 km east of Edmonton city centre, 4 km south of Wye Road on Rge. Rd. 231

SUGGESTED FIRST-TIME VIEWING:
1.5 hrs to walk the trail

THINGS TO DO:

- look for interesting bird behaviour from a wildlife-viewing stand at the small pond
- visit nearby Bretona Pond, just south of Hwy. 14, to watch waterfowl and other marsh birds

Walk into this densely wooded natural area and you'll feel as if you're many kilometres away from the city. Some of the forest is over 200 years old, with towering poplar and spruce giving you a sheltered, protected feeling. Here you can ease away everyday worries, and fill your senses with the beauty and wonders of each season.

Sherwood Park Natural Area is a 63-ha wildlife and woodland oasis surrounded by agricultural and residential land. Sitting on the western edge of the Beaver Hills, it's a rolling landscape with poplar and spruce forest, peatlands and swampy areas and a small pond surrounded by marsh.

Special features

Much of this natural area is mature poplar forest—a habitat frequented by owls and woodpeckers.

GREAT HORNED OWL

The great horned owl begins nesting early in March, often using the abandoned nest of a hawk. Look for a large twig nest sitting high in a poplar tree and check for the feather "horns" peeking over the edge. If you spot them, a new brood of owlets is on the way. Northern saw-whet owls are especially common, nesting in old woodpecker holes. If you're lucky, you might just see a little head poking out of a cavity. The mating call of the saw-whet is heard over and over in the spring, sounding like the high-pitched "beep" of trucks as they back up. The pileated woodpecker, a crow-sized and boldly painted bird, chips out large oblong holes near the base of trees looking for carpenter ants and insect larvae. (mature forest)

In the spring, along wet areas of the trail, listen for the "quacking" of wood frogs. They are

Sherwood Park

216

Sherwood Park Fwy.

630 · Wye Road

N

R.R. 231

Whitemud Drive

628

Sherwood Park Natural Area P

14

21

14

Bretona Pond P

0 · 5 km

sometimes mistaken for ducks in a flock. The boreal chorus frog makes a completely different call, which is like the sound you make running your fingernail along the teeth of a comb. (wet areas or pond)

BEAKED HAZELNUT

In the late summer and fall, shrubs that line the lower stretch of trail near the parking lot are laden with fruit: raspberry, pin cherry, beaked hazelnut, saskatoon, prickly rose, red-osier dogwood and choke cherry. These shrubs provide a food source for wildlife and make a colourful addition to the scenery.

The Old Edmonton Trail intersects the hiking trail in a couple of places. Until the 1940s, this road was used heavily by wagon trains moving coal, grain, mine props, lumber, cattle feed and other supplies between the Cooking Lake area and Edmonton. Two of the original survey markers are mounted as plaques for viewing along the hiking trail.

FOR MORE INFORMATION, CONTACT:
Alberta Community Development, Parks and Protected Areas
Phone (toll free):
1-866-427-3582
Web: www.cd.gov.ab.ca/ enjoying_alberta/parks/

Strathcona

LOCATION:
34 km east of Edmonton city centre

SUGGESTED FIRST-TIME VIEWING:
1.5 hours to explore the black spruce bog on Owl Trail

THINGS TO DO:

- register for an exciting range of outdoor education programs for individuals, families or groups in every season
- book the lodge as a retreat for your group
- rent skis, snowshoes and canoes at reasonable prices.

Note: fees are charged for facility bookings and ski trail passes.

Just a short drive from the city gets you to over 12 km of trails for exploring moose meadows, beaver crossings and Bennett Lake. This publicly operated facility promotes recreation and education in the outdoors but also preserves the environment. A special reason to visit is to explore an easily reached spruce bog. A boardwalk, constructed by the Timber Trekkers troop of the Junior Forest Wardens, takes you right into the midst of this interesting habitat.

Special features

Take the Owl Trail to reach the boardwalk that leads into the black spruce bog. The interior of a spruce forest is well protected from wind, rain and snow by the dense canopy of evergreen needles. Moose and deer often bed down here during extreme weather conditions. Porcupines, red squirrels and birds such as the red-breasted nuthatch use this habitat to feed, nest and raise young.

The black spruce, with its spindly trunk and irregular limbs, is not your ideal Christmas tree. Look for a club-shaped cluster of dense branches at the top of older trees. This species has an interesting way of reproducing itself. When the lower branches touch the ground and become covered with moss, roots develop and a new tree forms. The cones of the black spruce can withstand the heat of a fire and (like those of jack pine) will open after being scorched.

The floor of the spruce bog is cool and spongy. There is little light and the fallen needles create an acidic soil as they decompose. Only certain plants are able to grow in this environment. Look for

RED-BREASTED NUTHATCH

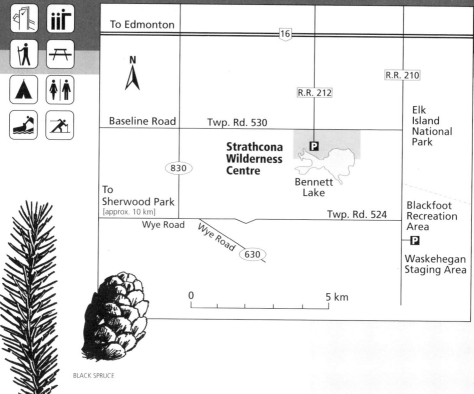

To Edmonton · 16

N

R.R. 210

R.R. 212

Elk Island National Park

Baseline Road · Twp. Rd. 530

Strathcona Wilderness Centre

P

830

Bennett Lake

To Sherwood Park
[approx. 10 km]

Twp. Rd. 524

Blackfoot Recreation Area

P

Wye Road · Wye Road

630

Waskehegan Staging Area

0 · 5 km

BLACK SPRUCE

Labrador tea. It has curled edges on its leathery leaves that persist all year round. Check the undersides, which are woolly and rust-coloured. The leaves make a strong-flavoured tea.

In the lowest areas, where the forest floor is very wet, you'll find sphagnum or peat moss. Sphagnum acts like a giant sponge, soaking up 20 times its own weight in water. Take a close look to see the intricate detail of this moss.

Old man's beard is a wispy lichen that hangs eerily from the coniferous trees. A lichen consists of two organisms: a fungus and an alga. The fungus provides a home for the alga, which by itself converts sunlight into food. Together, they form a winning team.

LABRADOR TEA

FOR MORE INFORMATION, CONTACT:
Strathcona Wilderness Centre
Phone: (780) 922-3939
Web: www.strathcona.ab.ca

55

Telford Lake

[LEDUC]

LOCATION:
35 km south of Edmonton city centre, at the east side of Leduc

SUGGESTED FIRST-TIME VIEWING:
1.5 hours to walk the lakeshore trail

THINGS TO DO:
- visit the Wood's House Museum for an audiotape tour of life during the Roaring Twenties. It's just a block west on 49th Ave.
- campers at Leduc Lions Campground in southeast Leduc can travel north along the trail system to Telford Lake.

Who would think that right on the edge of residential Leduc, there sits a haven for aquatic wildlife? Stroll down the long boardwalk to get a clear view of the lake. A 5-km asphalt trail skirts the lake edge, weaving past willows, aspen woods and lakeshore vegetation. Along the way, lean on the railing of an observation platform, read the interpretive signs and enjoy the sights. Wildlife species are partial to lake edges, so you'll find lots of birds and water critters here.

Special features

Cattails are the first thing you'll notice as you approach the lake. As soon as you see their hotdog-shaped seed heads, you know you're about to enter marsh habitat. The leaves of the cattail are used by birds to build nests and by muskrats to build lodges. Muskrats also eat marsh vegetation, including the leaves of the arrowhead plant, which is rooted in the mud at the lake edge and produces attractive white flowers, some of which become clusters of green fruit.

You'll likely spot the male red-winged blackbird straight away, as he shows his stuff, balancing on top of a cattail. Now, look carefully for a marsh wren. Since they spend most of their lives hidden in the reeds, these wrens can be difficult to spot. But you are likely to hear the male's song—a loud rattle coming from within the reeds. The marsh wren builds a round nest woven into the supporting stems of marsh plants, with an entrance on the side. The male will often build a few dummy nests to confuse predators.

RED-WINGED BLACKBIRD

Scoop up a handful of the lake water and look closely for tiny animal life. These mini-beasts are food for larger insects, fish, frogs, snakes and

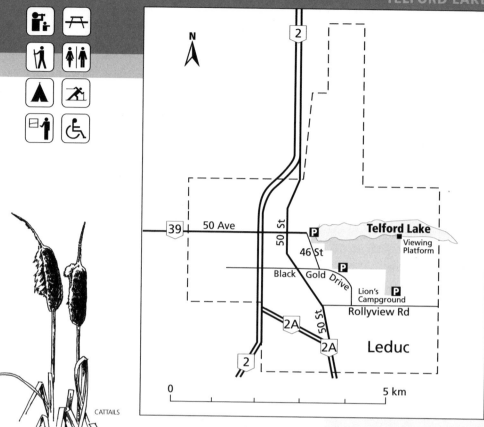

CATTAILS

waterfowl. Look closer still and you should be able to see the beating of a large oval heart through the transparent outer shell of a water flea.

It makes good sense to preserve Telford Lake when you see the hundreds of ducks and geese that stop here during spring and fall migrations. In spring plumage, the male mallard sports a glossy green head, white collar and chestnut breast. Later in the summer, the feathers begin to moult and the male then resembles the female with its mottled brown colour. During this moulting period, most ducks are unable to fly and must stay in deep water or hide in the reeds to escape predators.

WATER STRIDER

FOR MORE INFORMATION, CONTACT:
City of Leduc
Phone : (780) 980-7177
Web: www.city.leduc.ab.ca

57

Battle Lake

[AUTO TOUR]

DISTANCE:
238 km round trip from the Clifford E. Lee Nature Sanctuary

DRIVING TIME WITH NO STOPS:
3.5 hours

This all-day drive explores a portion of the scenic region around the North Saskatchewan River and the Battle Lake area, southwest of Edmonton. Take your time to enjoy the varied landscapes of deep river valleys mixed with rolling farmland and mixed-wood forests. The tour starts and ends at the Clifford E. Lee Nature Sanctuary (see page 22, which can be reached from Edmonton via Highway 16 heading west, and south on Highway 60 to Woodbend Road. A start from Edmonton would add about 50 km (round trip) to the tour from the west end of the city.

Stop #1 – Clifford E. Lee Nature Sanctuary

The sanctuary is reached from Hwy 60 by turning west on Woodbend Road (Twp. Rd. 514) and driving 1.5 km to Sanctuary Road, turning south and driving 1.2 km to the sanctuary on the west side of the road. Leave your vehicle in the parking lot and explore the board walk trails to discover the mysteries and variety of wildlife found in and around a marsh, as described on page 22.

Stop #2 – Hasse Lake Provincial Park

Return to Woodbend Road and drive 8.2 km west to the Golden Spike Road. Turn north and drive 3.0 km to Hwy 627, where you turn west and drive 20.7 km to Hwy 770. Turn north and drive 6.4 km to Twp. Rd. 524, turn east and follow the signs to Hasse Lake Provincial Park (see page 28). Explore the shoreline and forest and perhaps wet a fishing line for rainbow trout. If you plan to fish, check the current regulations guide.

Stop #3 – Genesee Bridge

Backtrack to Hwy 770 and drive south to where the road turns west and begins a steep descent into the valley of the North Saskatchewan River. Continue to Genesee Bridge, cross the river, and immediately after the bridge, take the first turnoff on the left that leads you to a boat launch. This is a good place to explore the anglers' trails along

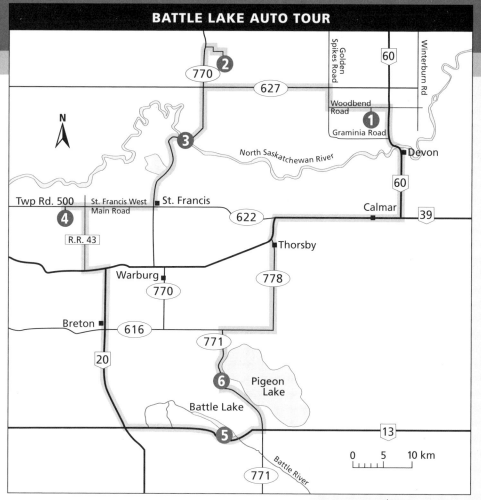

BATTLE LAKE AUTO TOUR

Golden Spikes Road
Winterburn Rd
60
627
Woodbend Road
1
Graminia Road
Devon
60
North Saskatchewan River
N
Twp Rd. 500
St. Francis West Main Road
St. Francis
622
Calmar
39
R.R. 43
Thorsby
Warburg
770
778
Breton
616
771
20
6
Pigeon Lake
Battle Lake
5
13
0   5   10 km
771
Battle River
2
770

1. Clifford E. Lee Nature Sanctuary
2. Hasse Lake Provincial Park
3. Genesee Bridge
4. Coyote Lake Nature Sanctuary
5. Battle Lake
6. Pigeon Lake Provincial Park

BRACKET FUNGI

59

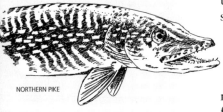

NORTHERN PIKE

the river and see a variety of waterfowl and shorebirds, as well as the occasional eagle. A diversity of fish—including northern pike, walleye, goldeye and sturgeon—inhabit the river, and can be fished from shore. If you plan to fish, check the current regulations guide for restrictions specific to this river. Be aware that flowing water can be deceptively dangerous. Keep children and pets out of the water or off the river ice!

Stop #4 – Coyote Lake Nature Sanctuary

Continue west and then south on Hwy 770 out of the river valley, on past the Epcor Genesee coal-fired power plant and over the bridge crossing the haul road for the coal mine. Just past this bridge is the plant cooling pond (Genesee Lake) which is home to a variety of waterfowl, shorebirds, and red-winged and yellow-headed blackbirds. Unfortunately, there is no turnout or parking area here, and access to the pond is prohibited. So, if you slow down to view the birds, make sure you are not impeding traffic. Continue on to the community of St. Francis (14.3 km from Genesee Bridge) and the junction with Hwy 622 (which heads east). At the junction, turn west on Twp. Rd. 500 and drive 12.9 km to the Coyote Lake turnoff (Rge. Rd. 44). Continue to the sanctuary, register at a box outside the stewards' house and pick up a brochure. Then park your vehicle at the designated lot by the picnic area. See page 24 or things to do and special features about this unique sanctuary.

Stop #5 – Battle Lake

Return to Twp. Rd. 500 and drive east 1.6 km to Rge. Rd. 43. Turn south, initially skirting the east boundary of the Coyote Lake Nature Sanctuary, and drive 10.4 km to Hwy 39. Turn east and drive 3.2 km to the community of Alsike and the junction with Hwy 20. Turn south and drive 26.5 km to the junction with Hwy 13. Turn east, driving 16.8 km to the turnoff on the north side of the road to the Alberta 4-H Centre on Battle Lake. See page 18 for things to do at the centre and on the lake. Battle Lake is the headwaters of the Battle River.

Stop #6 – Pigeon Lake Provincial Park

From the 4-H centre, return to Hwy 13 and continue east 5.4 km across the Battle River to Rge. Rd. 14, the turnoff to Battle Lake Park (4.9 km). Managed by the County of Wetaskiwin, the park includes camping and picnic areas and a boat launch. Continue on Hwy 13, 1.6 km to its junction with Hwy 771. Turn north and drive 8.5 km to Pigeon Lake Provincial Park. Drive into the privately managed campground, and at the gate, request a brochure showing the hiking trails located west of the campground. These broad, easily walked trails take you through mixed-wood forest to overlooks of meadow and wetland where you can see a variety of bird and mammal life. The park also provides boat access to Pigeon Lake where you can angle for a variety of fish, including walleye, perch and pike. Special fishing regulations apply to this lake.

From Pigeon Lake, there are several ways to return to Edmonton. The quickest and most direct is to backtrack to Hwy 13 and drive east to Hwy 2 and then north to Edmonton. A more leisurely and scenic route is to continue north on Hwy 771, as it skirts the west shore of Pigeon Lake, to Hwy 616. Turn east and drive 8.1 km to Hwy 778. Turn north and drive 15.1 km to the town of Thorsby and the junction with Hwy 39. Turn east and drive 23.8 km through Calmar to Hwy 60. Here you can either go north, crossing the North Saskatchewan River near Devon, to Woodbend Road (and the start of the tour) and on to Edmonton; or go east on Hwy 39 to Hwy 2 and north to Edmonton.

MULE DEER

61

Big Lake – Matchayaw Lake

[AUTO TOUR]

DISTANCE:
104 km round trip from St. Albert

DRIVING TIME WITH NO STOPS:
1.5 hours

This relatively short excursion into the rolling farm and lake country west of Edmonton is a pleasant drive just made for a leisurely Sunday afternoon. The tour begins in St. Albert on the north side of the Sturgeon River. Take Mission Avenue southwest to where Meadowview Drive begins at the railroad track. A start from Edmonton would add about 25 km (round trip) to the tour from the centre of the city.

Stop #1 – Big Lake Interpretive Trail

Drive 7.2 km down Meadowview Drive from the railroad track in St. Albert. On the way, you'll see glimpses of Big Lake to your left. Big Lake is surrounded by private land and there are just a few points for public access. At kilometre 5.5 you cross the bridge over the Sturgeon River entering Big Lake and forming the delta that nearly divides the lake in two. Continue on to kilometre 7.2 where a sign on the left identifies the Big Lake Interpretive Trail. Park in the designated area and walk the trail as described on page 32.

Stop #2 – Imrie Park on Matchayaw Lake

Continue about 5 km west on Meadowview Drive to Hwy 44 (Rge. Rd. 265). Turn north and drive 12 km to Hwy 37. Turn west and drive 21.8 km to Rge. Rd. 15. As you approach the road, you see Matchayaw Lake (locally known as Devil's Lake) appear on the left, and a road heading back east along the north and east shore of the lake to a public boat launch and other developments. Rge. Rd. 15 is just beyond this road on Hwy 37. Turn south heading down the west side of the lake and drive 1.2 km to Imrie Park on the left. The park is a great

FRANKLIN'S GULL

BIG LAKE – MATCHAYAW LAKE AUTO TOUR

1 Big Lake Interpretive Trail

2 Imrie Park on Matchayaw Lake

3 Bilby Natural Area

4 Chickakoo Lake

5 Wagner Natural Area

PRICKLY ROSE

place to hike and watch waterfowl and other wildlife, as described on page 30.

Stop #3 – Bilby Natural Area

Drive 1.6 km south on Rge. Rd. 15 across the railroad track to the Bilby Provincial Natural Area. A gate and sign mark the area on the east side of the road. Park on the side of the road and enter the area through the pedestrian gate to the left of the locked gate that prevents access to motorized vehicles. Follow the undeveloped trails around the beaver ponds on Kilini Creek where there are good chances to see red-winged blackbirds, mallards, goldeneyes, as well as blue jays, ruffed grouse and red squirrels.

Stop #4 – Chickakoo Lake

Continue 1.2 km south on Rge. Rd. 15 to Twp. Rd. 544. Turn east and drive 1.6 km to Rge. Rd. 14, turn south and drive 6.4 km to Twp. Rd. 540. Turn east and drive 1.5 km to Rge. Rd. 13, where you turn south and drive 1.9 km to the Chickakoo Lake Recreation Area. Take one of the many enjoyable trails around the lakes and ponds as described on page 20. Chickakoo Lake is annually stocked with eastern brook trout. If you plan to fish, check the current regulations guide.

BROOK TROUT

Stop #5 – Wagner Natural Area

Return to Rge. Rd. 13 and drive south 2.1 km to Twp. Rd. 534. Turn east, and drive 4.1 km to Hwy 779 (Rge. Rd. 10). Turn south and drive 3.2 km to Hwy 16. Drive 11.1 km east on Hwy 16 to Atim Rd (Rge. Rd. 270). Turn south and immediately east into the parking area of the Wagner Natural Area. Take the 1.2 km trail and boardwalk through the fascinating worlds of fens, ponds and muskegs, as described on page 36.

Return to Edmonton or St. Albert via Hwy. 16.

MARSH MARIGOLD

NORTHERN PINTAIL

Wabamun Lake– Lac Ste. Anne

This scenic drive takes you alongside three large lakes west of Edmonton. In between, you'll drive a landscape with a mix of rolling farmland and poplar and spruce forest. This tour starts and ends at Wabamun Lake Provincial Park, but you can also start the tour from Edmonton via Highways 16 or 16A, or Hwy. 627. An Edmonton starting-point will add about 125 km (round trip) to the tour.

DISTANCE:
100 km round trip from Wabamun Lake Provincial Park

DRIVING TIME WITH NO STOPS:
2 hours

Stop #1 – Wabamun Lake Provincial Park

The exit from Hwy. 16 to the park (Kapasiwin turnoff) is well-marked as you approach from the east. The access to the park is on your right a short distance south of the highway. Scan Moonlight Bay or go for a short hike along park trails. Check page 34 for detailed information.

Stop #2 – Wabamun Town Dock

Return to Hwy. 16, travel a few kilometres further west and turn south at the overpass to the Wabamun Town site. Continue through town to the parking and day use area near the dock. Scan the large marsh between the dock and Point Alison. The water from the Wabamun power plant keeps this part of the lake open year-round. Look for eagles on the larger trees on Point Alison (winter).

Stop #3 – East Pit Lake

Return to Hwy 16 and take the overpass across the highway. Drive 1.1 km north to a parking lot on the left (west) side of the road. Park here as no vehicles are allowed beyond this point. After reading the sign describing rules of use, take the short trail over the ridge to this pleasing, long and narrow lake that is a reclaimed coal mining pit. The lake is stocked annually with rainbow trout, and the Stony Plain Fish and Game Club manages the habitat development surrounding the lake, including nesting platforms and boxes

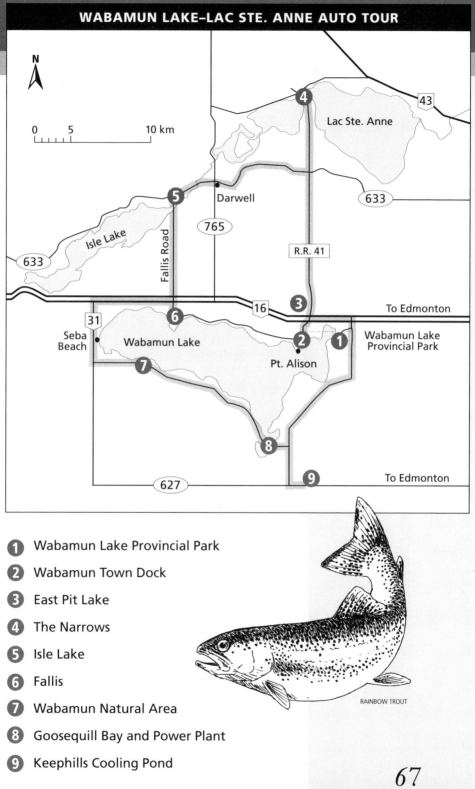

WABAMUN LAKE–LAC STE. ANNE AUTO TOUR

N

0   5   10 km

43

Lac Ste. Anne

Darwell

633

765

Isle Lake

633

Fallis Road

R.R. 41

16

To Edmonton

31

Seba Beach

Wabamun Lake

Pt. Alison

Wabamun Lake Provincial Park

Wabamun Natural Area

Goosequill Bay and Power Plant

627

To Edmonton

1 Wabamun Lake Provincial Park

2 Wabamun Town Dock

3 East Pit Lake

4 The Narrows

5 Isle Lake

6 Fallis

7 Wabamun Natural Area

8 Goosequill Bay and Power Plant

9 Keephills Cooling Pond

RAINBOW TROUT

for several species of birds. If you plan to fish, check the current regulations guide.

Stop #4 – The Narrows

Continue north on the road (Rge. Rd. 41) past the Whitewood mine to the Narrows on Lac Ste. Anne (16.7 km). Watch for ospreys on towers along the power line. The Narrows, which joins the two parts of Lac Ste. Anne, is a favourite fishing spot for both anglers and water birds such as grebes. If you plan to fish, check the current regulations guide for restrictions specific to this lake.

Stop #5 – Isle Lake

GRAY JAY

Backtrack south to Hwy. 633 and turn west. Drive 9 km west to the Fallis Road (3.2 km past the community of Darwell), then turn south and within 1 km you will pass over a bridge at the east end of Isle Lake. You can stop here at Baybridge Park, which has picnic tables and pit toilets. This part of Isle Lake is shallow and marshy and there are usually lots of water birds visible from the road. You may be lucky enough to see gray jays near the picnic site— looking for scraps of leftover food. Isle Lake forms a part of the headwaters of the Sturgeon River, which flows into Lac Ste. Anne, Big Lake and eventually the North Saskatchewan River near Fort Saskatchewan. Continue south on the Fallis Road to Hwy. 16.

Stop #6 – Fallis

Continue south across Hwy. 16 at Fallis and onto a hill overlooking Wabamun Lake's Coal Point. There is a wide spot to pull off near the top of the hill. You can see the Sundance and Keephills Power Plants and the mine across the lake. Look for ospreys on the artificial nest platform visible near the spruce trees on the west side of Coal Point. (At this point the route can be shortened by following the north shore road eastward, back to the Wabamun town site. Continue east down the hill and along the lakeshore. Watch for ospreys along the north shore of the lake. An exposure of brick-red shale occurs on the north side of the road, the result of a burnt-out coal seam.)

Stop #7 – Wabamun Natural Area

Return to Fallis at Hwy. 16, turn west and drive to the Seba Beach turnoff at Hwy. 31. Head south past Seba Beach, then east on Sundance Road to the Wabamun Natural Area (4.0 km from the corner). This site is at a higher elevation than the lake and so it features different plants and animals than seen along the shore. The natural area has no facilities and is not well-marked, but it is definitely worth a short stop.

Stop #8 – Goosequill Bay and Power Plant

Follow the road past the Sundance Power Plant to Goosequill Bay. This large shallow marsh usually has numerous birds. The cooling pond behind the dyke to the southwest of the road is a good spot to view overwintering waterfowl.

Stop #9 – Keephills Cooling Pond

Continue further east to a T-intersection, then turn right to get to Keephills Cooling Pond. You can return to Edmonton via Hwy. 627, or else backtrack north and go through the Wabamun Indian Reserve to the provincial park and Hwy. 16. If you follow Hwy. 627, note the deep valley of Wabamun Creek, with its growth of spruce forest. You will also get a good view of the North Saskatchewan River Valley near the site of an early fur-trading post, Upper White Mud House.

COMMON MERGANSER

69

Cooking Lake Moraine

DISTANCE:
110 km round trip from
southeast city limits

**DRIVING TIME
WITH NO STOPS:**
2.2 hours

The Cooking Lake Moraine makes for an interesting drive on roads that wind over hills and into hollows of this hummocky landscape. About 10 000 years ago, huge blocks of ice encrusted with silt, sand and gravel broke off from melting glaciers. As these buried blocks of ice melted, they left hills and hollows, which are now forested ridges and water bodies.

Stop #1 – Sherwood Park Natural Area

Leave Edmonton via Sherwood Park Freeway and drive to Rge. Rd. 231 on the east side of Sherwood Park. Turn right and drive south 4 km to the natural area. Stop in the parking lot on your right. Glance over the interpretive trailhead signs for an overview. If you're intrigued, and time allows, walk the trail of this heavily wooded site. It lies on the western edge of the Cooking Lake Moraine. Check page 52 for detailed information.

Stop #2 – Bretona Pond

Continue 2.5 km farther south on Rge. Rd. 231 and then 3 km west on Hwy. 14. Turn south at the Watchable Wildlife sign, then turn right into a parking area. This site is Bretona Pond—a Buck for Wildlife habitat development site. A short walk will take you to the floating dock and viewing area. Most waterfowl will stay on the west side of the pond, so a pair of binoculars will come in handy. Scan for eared grebes, black terns, tree swallows and red-winged blackbirds.

When you leave Bretona Pond, drive 14 km east on Hwy. 14. Be on the lookout for bird boxes on fence posts along the highway. Tree swallows and mountain bluebirds use these boxes for raising young.

Stop #3 – South Cooking Lake

Turn left into town and follow the day use picnic table signs to South Cooking Lake Park. Walk

COOKING LAKE MORAINE AUTO TOUR

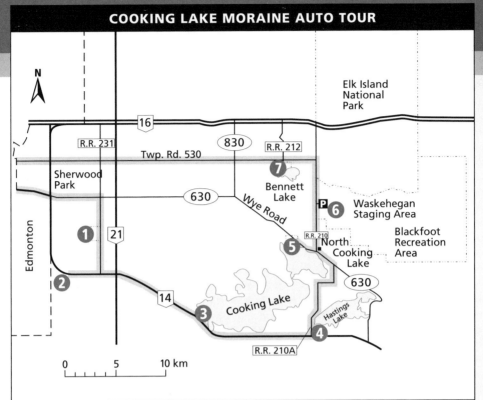

Map labels:
- N
- Elk Island National Park
- 16
- R.R. 231
- 830
- R.R. 212
- Twp. Rd. 530
- Sherwood Park
- Bennett Lake
- 630
- Wye Road
- P
- Waskehegan Staging Area
- Edmonton
- 21
- 1
- North Cooking Lake
- R.R. 210
- Blackfoot Recreation Area
- 5
- 2
- 14
- 630
- 3
- Cooking Lake
- Hastings Lake
- 4
- R.R. 210A
- 0   5   10 km

1. Sherwood Park Natural Area
2. Bretona Pond
3. South Cooking Lake
4. Hastings Lake
5. North Cooking Lake Natural Area
6. Blackfoot Recreation Area
7. Strathcona Wilderness Centre

BLACK TERN

71

down to the lake and look for waterfowl, eared grebes, canvasbacks, ring-necked ducks and Canada geese. Bald eagles pass through in spring and fall.

When you get back to the highway, turn left and continue east. You'll cross a marsh, which is a shallow bay of Cooking Lake. Watch for Canada geese and the exotic-looking yellow-headed blackbird. The road then curves left around the lake. Take the moose-crossing sign seriously because there are plenty of moose and white-tailed deer in the area. You will then be driving through the middle of the Cooking Lake Moraine and will notice many ponds along the road. Most contain waterfowl and some of the larger ponds have a beaver lodge.

Stop #4 – Hastings Lake
After driving 13 km, turn left at the Deville sign onto Rge. Rd. 210A. Within 2 km, you'll see Hastings Lake on your right where there is room to pull off the road. The west end of the lake is shallow and attracts lots of waterfowl. American white pelicans, terns and double-crested cormorants use this lake for fishing. Western grebes nest in a colony in the offshore reed beds.

Stop #5 – North Cooking Lake Natural Area
Continue north on this road for about 4 km through the ranching country between Cooking and Hastings lakes. Continue to Hwy. 630 and follow it to the west. About 3.5 km past the hamlet of North Cooking Lake there is a natural area parking lot on your left. (Note: parking lot is at intersection of Twp. Rd. 522 and Hwy. 630.) If you feel energetic, hike the wetlands trail to the shore of Cooking Lake (about 1 hour). Wear good hiking or rubber boots since the trail is rough and often wet. The trail traces

more than 1.5 km of shoreline, with aspen forest, ponds, meadows and wetlands along the way. In June, July and August, look for the world's smallest flowering plant—ducksmeal. It resembles green grains floating on the water's surface. Puddle ducks like mallards and blue-winged teal scoop these plants from the water.

If you're running out of time, head back to Edmonton on Wye Road (Secondary Hwy. 630).

Stop #6 – Blackfoot Recreation Area
Drive back to the hamlet of North Cooking Lake and turn north on Rge. Rd. 210. Drive 4.6 km, watch for the signs and turn right into the Waskehegan Staging Area. You could stop here for a meal at the picnic shelter—or stretch your legs on a trail. Check page 42 for detailed information, or stop at the park office for current brochures.

Stop #7 – Strathcona Wilderness Centre
Continue driving north on Rge. Rd. 210 along the west fence line of the Blackfoot Recreation Area, which then becomes the boundary of Elk Island National Park. Look for wood bison that frequently graze along this fence line. Don't get out of your vehicle to approach the bison; they may charge at you. After 4 km, turn west along Baseline Road (Twp. Rd. 530). After about 3 km, look for signs and a large gate entrance leading from the south side of the road and into the Strathcona Wilderness Centre. Check in at the centre to enquire about events. Check page 54 for detailed information.

To return to Edmonton, continue west on Baseline Road for about 30 km.

MOUNTAIN BLUEBIRD

Gwynne Outlet

[AUTO TOUR]

DISTANCE:
190 km (round trip from south city limits)

DRIVING TIME WITH NO STOPS:
2.5 hours or less

During the time that glaciers covered much of Alberta, some ice and debris blocked the flow of water from melting glaciers, damming a huge lake that covered the Edmonton area. The water broke through the ice-dam and escaped to the south in a raging flood. In a matter of days, the water scoured a valley, as much as 50 m deep and 1 km wide, now called the Gwynne Outlet. Saunders, Ord and Coal lakes still hold water in the valley of this ancient melt-water spillway.

Stop #1 – Telford Lake

Drive 16 km south of Edmonton on Hwy. 2 to Leduc. Take the Calmar/Drayton Valley exit and turn east to Leduc centre. Follow 50th Ave. over the railway tracks, turn right on 46th Street, then immediately left into the Telford House parking lot. Telford Lake is a side channel of the Gwynne Outlet. Get a good view of the lake from the boardwalk. Watch for red-necked grebes, gadwalls, ring-necked ducks, Canada geese, blue-winged teals, ruddy ducks and eared grebes. Check page 56 for detailed information.

Stop #2 – Saunders Lake

Go back on 50th Ave. to 50th St. and turn south to Hwy. 623. Turn east and drive to the south end of Saunders Lake, about 7 km. Park near the top of the hill on Rge. Rd. 243. Be careful of traffic as you walk down the hill. This lake lies in the Gwynne Outlet channel. As far as you can see, this valley extends north and south. Imagine how it looked about 12 000 years ago, when the outlet carried a thousand times the water flow of the North Saskatchewan River.

Stop #3 – Coal Lake, north end

Upon leaving Saunders Lake, drive east 1 km past farmland and rolling hills. Turn south on Hwy. 814 and drive 13 km. Then turn east on Hwy. 616 and drive about 4 km. The large valley ahead is

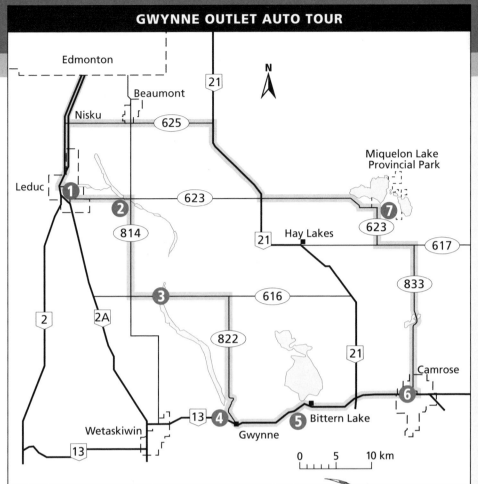

GWYNNE OUTLET AUTO TOUR

Edmonton

Beaumont

Nisku

21

625

Leduc

1

2

814

623

Miquelon Lake
Provincial Park

7

623

21 Hay Lakes

617

833

3

616

2

2A

822

21

Camrose

6

13 **4**

5 Bittern Lake

Wetaskiwin

Gwynne

13

0   5   10 km

N

1 Telford Lake

2 Saunders Lake

3 Coal Lake, north end

4 Coal Lake, south end

5 Bittern Lake

6 Camrose Municipal Park

7 Miquelon Lake Provincial Park

MARSH REED GRASS

75

the Gwynne Outlet again, with Coal Lake nestled in the bottom. Drive down to a provincial campground in the valley bottom. The lake has good fishing for yellow perch and northern pike. You can also expect to see fish-eating birds such as terns, cormorants and pelicans. If the kids have energy to burn, explore the trails and woods that border this narrow lake.

Stop #4 – Coal Lake, south end

Follow Hwy. 616 to the east, up and out of the valley, and drive just over 8 km to Hwy. 822. Set your odometer, since Hwy. 822 is not marked. Look for hawks such as the Swainson's hawk sitting on fence posts. Also watch for ducks and shorebirds at several wetlands along this road. Turn south on Rge. Rd. 230 (Hwy. 822) and drive 15 km to another campground at the south end of Coal Lake. A dam across this end of the lake controls the water level. Look for common goldeneye and other ducks.

Stop #5 – Bittern Lake

Travel a couple more kilometres south and you hit Hwy. 13. Turn east toward Bittern Lake. As you leave the Gwynne Outlet channel, you pass the town of Gwynne on the south side of the road. After 8 km, watch for the Bittern Lake Campsite to the south. Look for shorebirds and waterfowl on the alkaline wetlands around the campsite. Bittern Lake itself is difficult to reach, but you can get a good (though distant) view of the lake from the first road to the north, about 1 km east of the campground.

Stop #6 – Camrose Municipal Park

Follow Hwy. 13 east for 13 km to Camrose. Just a few blocks into town, you'll see an

Information Centre on the north side of the road, which is adjacent Mirror Lake. Stop to view the displays and get current information. Walk the trails leading from the centre and look for the trumpeter swans that are kept in the park year-round. These birds were used to breed some of the trumpeter swans re-introduced into Elk Island National Park.

Stop #7 – Miquelon Lake Provincial Park

Turn north on 51st Street just past Mirror Lake and then go west to 53rd Street. Follow that street north where it becomes Hwy. 833. About 7 km out of town, the road angles around several sloughs. Check for waterfowl activity. Another 9 km will bring you to Hwy. 617. Turn west and travel 5 km to Hwy. 623; turn north and continue about 5 km along the road to Miquelon Lake. Park just past the permit booth on the right side of the road. A short paved trail follows the shoreline of Grebe Pond. A large beaver lodge sits smack in the centre of the pond and red-necked grebes are never far from view. Check page 50 for detailed information.

Follow Hwy. 623 west from Miquelon Lake Provincial Park to Hwy. 21 and turn north. When you reach Hwy. 625, turn west and drive 20 km to Hwy. 2. After you pass Beaumont and just before Nisku, you'll drive through a wide, shallow valley. This valley is your farewell view of the Gwynne Outlet. Continue to Nisku, then north on Hwy. 2 to Edmonton.

EARED GREBE

77

Sources for Further Information

Agency and Organization Contacts

The following agencies and organizations are knowledgeable sources of information, including site-specific natural history information.

Alberta Sustainable Resource Development Information Centre, Main Floor, 9920-108 Street, Edmonton, T5K 2M4; Phone: (780) 944-0313; Web: www3.gov.ab.ca/srd/info

Alberta Fish and Game Association, 6924-104 Street, Edmonton, T6H 2L7; Phone: (780) 437-2342; Web: www.afga.org

Beaverhill Lake Nature Centre, Town of Tofield, Box 30, Tofield, T0B 4J0; Phone: (780) 662-3191; Web: www.tofieldalberta.ca/nature.htm

Edmonton Bird Club, Box 1111, Edmonton, T5J 2M1; Web: www.ebc.fanweb.ca

Edmonton Geological Society, c/o Dept. of Geology, University of Alberta, Edmonton, T6G 2E3; Web: www.egs.ab.ca

Edmonton Natural History Club, Box 1582, Edmonton, T5J 2N9; Web: www.fanweb.ca

Elk Island National Park, Site 4, R.R. #1, Fort Saskatchewan, T8L 2N7; Phone: 992-2950; Web: www.parkscanada.gc.ca/

Federation of Alberta Naturalists, 11759 - Groat Road, Edmonton, Alberta T5M 3K6; Phone: (780) 427-8124; Web: www.fanweb.ca

Parks and Protected Areas, Alberta Community Development; Phone (toll free): 1-866-427-3582; Web: www.cd.gov.ab.ca/enjoying_alberta/parks

Provincial Museum of Alberta, 12845-102 Avenue, Edmonton, T5N 0M6; Phone: 453-9100; Web: www.pma.edmonton.ab.ca

John Janzen Nature Centre, The City of Edmonton, P.O. Box 2359, Edmonton, T5J 2R7; Phone: (780) 496-2925; Web: through www.gov.edmonton.ab.ca

River Valley Centre, The City of Edmonton; Phone: (780) 496-7275; Web: through www.gov.edmonton.ab.ca

Editor's Choice of References

The following publications provide basic information about various aspects of natural history of wildlife and plants, including identification. Each of these publications contains additional reference titles, which will allow you to understand better the interesting behavioural and ecological observations you make during your visits to wildlife-viewing sites in and around Edmonton.

These publications can be found through most libraries and many are available in book stores.

General Natural History:
Alberta Naturalist – quarterly publication of the Federation of Alberta Naturalists (see Agency and Organization Contacts above), available through the organization or libraries for back issues; natural history research and information; news about meetings, conferences and local affiliated clubs' activities.

Edmonton Naturalist – periodical publication of the Edmonton Natural History Club (see Contacts on p.78), available through the organization or libraries for back issues; natural history of plants and animals in the Edmonton area; news about meetings, and field activities.

Knee High Nature in Alberta – Winter 1988, (Fall 1989, Summer 1990, Spring 1991) – D. Hayley and P. Wishart. Knee High Nature, Sherwood Park; children-oriented books told simply, well-illustrated with drawings; focused on bringing children and parents together while doing activities.

Animals:
Alberta Mammals: An Atlas and Guide. 1993. H.C. Smith. The Provincial Museum of Alberta, Edmonton; brief descriptions of distribution, habitat and key identifying features of Alberta's 91 species of mammals; plots distribution on provincial-scale maps; skull drawings and measurements for the serious student of mammals; photographs.

Hoofed Mammals of Alberta. 1993. J.B. Stelfox (ed.). Lone Pine Publishing, Edmonton; comprehensive reference to Alberta's nine species of ungulates; includes identification based on tracks, skulls, scats, antlers and horns; reviews ecology, physiology, management; photographs.

Mammals of Alberta. 1999. D. Pattie and C. Fisher. Lone Pine Publishing, Edmonton; descriptions of 91 species including photographs.

A Winter Birding Guide for the Edmonton Region. 1988. Compiled by H. Stelfox and C. Fisher. Edmonton Natural History Club; a comprehensive guide to enjoying urban birding during Edmonton's winter season.

The Atlas of Breeding Birds of Alberta.1992. Federation of Alberta Naturalists, Edmonton; covers Alberta's 270 breeding birds, including their distribution, habitat and nesting preferences; detailed provincial-scale map of breeding records; photographs.

Birds of Alberta. 1998. C. C. Fisher and J. Acorn. Lone Pine Publishing, Edmonton; contains 332 common species plus 56 additional species, including 343 full-color illustrations.

Birds of Edmonton.1990. (revised). R. Bovey, Lone Pine Publishing, Edmonton; an introduction to Edmonton's more common species of birds; illustrations for identification of these species; discusses bird feeders, attracting birds, nest boxes and backyard habitat.

The Bugs of Alberta. 2000. J. Acorn and I. Sheldon. Lone Pine Publishing, Edmonton; descriptions of 125 species of insects with illustrations.

Field Guide to Animal Tracks. 1975. Olaus J. Murie. Houghton Mifflin. The classic, comprehensive guide to tracks and signs of animals of all kinds. Also includes notes on the natural history of many of these animals.

Field Guide to the Birds of North America. 1987. (second edition). National Geographic Society, Washington, D.C.; includes over 800 species that occur in North America; describes physical features, breeding habitats and seasonal distribution; small-scale maps; illustrations.

The Amphibians and Reptiles of Alberta. 1993. A.P. Russell and A.M. Bauer. University of Alberta Press, Edmonton, Alberta; detailed physical descriptions, natural history and distribution information; for each species, provincial-scale maps feature site records; photographs.

Fish of Alberta. 2003. A. Joynt and M.G. Sullivan. Lone Pine Publishing, Edmonton; 176 pages with color illustrations by I. Sheldon.

Fishes of Alberta. 1992. (second edition). J.S. Nelson and M.J. Paetz. The University of Alberta Press, Edmonton, Alberta; all 59 species of fish known to occur in Alberta are described; natural history and distribution are detailed;

provincial-scale maps with site records along watercourses and in water bodies; discusses management and taxonomy; photographs.

Butterflies of Alberta. 1993. J.H. Acorn. Lone Pine Publishing, Edmonton; detailed physical descriptions of butterflies occurring in Alberta; natural history information; focused on viewing of butterflies; photographs.

CANADIAN TIGER
SWALLOWTAIL

Plants:
Flora of Alberta. 1983. E.H. Moss. (second edition revised by J.G. Packer.) University of Toronto Press, Toronto; technical keys and descriptions of all ferns, fern allies and flowering plants known to occur in Alberta, apart from more recent records; distribution maps; for the more serious student of botany.

Mosses, Lichens & Ferns of Northwest North American. 1988. D.H. Vitt, J.E. Marsh and R.B. Bovey. Lone Pine Publishing, Edmonton; photographic field guide; distribution maps; ecological habitat guide; identification keys; general description.

Mushrooms of Western Canada. 1991. H.M.E. Schalkwijk-Barendsen. Lone Pine Publishing, Edmonton; illustrated identification guide; species descriptions; assessment of edibility.

Plants of the Western Boreal Forest and Aspen Parkland. 1995. D. Johnson, L. Kershaw, A. MacKinnon and J. Pojar. Lone Pine Publishing, Edmonton; beautifully illustrated and easy-to-use field guide to the full range of plant species.

Trees and Shrubs of Alberta. 1990. K. Wilkinson, Lone Pine Publishing, Edmonton, Alberta; detailed physical descriptions of 77 species; keys for identification; small-scale maps of distribution in province; photographs.

Wildflowers Across the Prairies. 1984. F.R. Vance, J.R. Jowsey and J.S. McLean. Western Producer Prairie Books,

Saskatoon, Saskatchewan; non-technical field guide to nearly 400 species of flowering plants; color photos and black-line sketches.

Wildflowers of Alberta. 1977. R.G.H. Cormack, Hurtig Publishers Ltd., Edmonton, Alberta; brief physical descriptions for identification of about 400 species of the more common wildflowers in Alberta; distribution is described; general information and uses discussed; photographs.

Wildflowers of Edmonton and Central Alberta. 1996. R. Dickinson and F. Royer, University of Alberta Press; descriptions of more than 140 common or characteristic flowering plants of Central Alberta, with 225 colour photos.

Viewing Sites:
Alberta Wildlife Viewing Guide. 1990. Alberta Forestry, Lands and Wildlife and Lone Pine Publishing, Edmonton; more than 60 wildlife-viewing sites are described; features information on access, seasonal viewing, key species and viewing practices; photographs. This guide is also on the web at www3.gov.ab.ca/srd/fw/view.

A Nature Guide to Alberta. 1980. Provincial Museum of Alberta Publication #5, Hurtig Publishers Ltd., Edmonton; describes wildlife and other natural features for 171 viewing locations in the province; information on access; regional maps with sites indicated; viewing ethics; photographs.

Land Reference Manual web site – www.cd.gov.ab.ca/preserving/parks/lrm/; a listing of all lands currently under the administration of Alberta Community Development, Parks and Protected Areas, including land descriptions and maps.

Edmonton Beneath Our Feet. 1993. J.D. Godfrey (ed.). Edmonton Geological Society, Edmonton (see Contacts on p.78); reviews basic geology of landforms, geological history, fossils, groundwater and soils of Edmonton area; discusses economic and practical aspects of geology; detailed viewing guide for geological features of North Saskatchewan River Valley trail.